Praise for *The Highly Effective Missionary*

"My son David was born with a Book of Mormon in one hand and a Preach My Gospel in the other. When it comes to missionary work, he has been a continual force for good in so many ways. David has always felt that missionaries needed to learn how to effectively deal with people, understand them, [and] walk in their shoes before trying to get them to change their lives. David knows what it takes to do this and his new book on missionary work is extraordinary! People skills are just one aspect of the myriad things you will learn to become a more effective missionary. I am proud of this book and proud of my son. Like Alma of old, I believe David will be a missionary "all the days of his life."

—Stephen R. Covey
Author, *The 7 Habits of Highly Effective People*

"As his former mission president, David treated the primary step in bringing souls to Christ with candor and true-life examples. They really work. I witnessed what he has written. This book is dynamic. It can work for you directly or with small adaptations to your missionary service."

—Ed J. Pinegar
Former mission president and MTC president

"The gospel doesn't change, but like almost everything else, the way we can effectively present it as full time and member missionaries changes a great deal with the times. Our good friend David Covey has captured in a succinct and very readable form just what many of these changes need to be!"

—Richard and Linda Eyre
#1 *New York Times* bestselling authors and former mission president of the England London South Mission

"Great ideas and useful tools for missionaries. I only wish I had read this sooner!"

—John Bytheway
Popular author, instructor, and motivational speaker

T0027277

"David Covey is a bold missionary! We can learn a lot from him as we stretch out of our comfort zones and become bolder ourselves. The suggestions he offers in this book provide a great starting point!"

—Brad Wilcox
Former mission president, mission prep teacher,
and author of *The Continuous Atonement*

"David Covey's accomplishments as a young, sweetly bold missionary were legendary. He now brings a seasoned reflection on those skills that fostered so much proselyting success. This book is filled with nuggets of practical insight."

—Matthew S. Holland
President, Utah Valley University

"The speed of missionary work has been hastened. This book will help those people preparing to serve missions be able to match that speed. I wish I could have read this before I served a mission."

—Chad Lewis
Three-time All Pro NFL tight end

"As mission president, I invited David Covey to come train my missionaries. I found David's approach literally changed the "mind-set" of my missionaries. After applying his excellent concepts, results began to roll in very quickly. In fact, even missionaries who were not naturally bold found that by learning these new skills and techniques, they greatly enhanced their success. David Covey has the best missionary approach I have ever seen."

—John Grove
Former mission president

"Nothing overstresses missionaries more than lack of success. The techniques in this book may initially take us out of our comfort zones, but they can draw the Comforter to us and those we teach. I wish I'd mastered more of these ideas as a young missionary!"

—Wendy Ulrich
LDS author and founder of Sixteen Stones Center for Growth

DAVID M. R. COVEY

THE HIGHLY EFFECTIVE MISSIONARY

Bold & Innovative Approaches to Hasten the Work

CFI
An Imprint of Cedar Fort, Inc.
Springville, Utah

ISBN 13: 978-1-4621-1230-2

Published by CFI, an imprint of Cedar Fort, Inc.
2373 W. 700 S., Springville, UT 84663
Distributed by Cedar Fort, Inc., www.cedarfort.com

LIBRARY OF CONGRESS CATALOGING-IN-PUBLICATION DATA

Covey, David M. R., 1966- author.
The highly effective missionary : a bold and innovative approach for today's missionary / David M.R. Covey.
    pages cm
Includes bibliographical references and index.
ISBN 978-1-4621-1230-2 (alk. paper)
1. Mormon missionaries--Training of. 2. Church of Jesus Christ of Latter-day Saints--Missions.
I. Title.

BX8661.C66 2013
266'.9332--dc23

2013018037

Cover design by Shawnda T. Craig
Cover design © 2013 Lyle Mortimer
Edited by Emily S. Chambers
Typeset by Valene Wood

Printed in the United States of America

10 9 8 7 6 5 4 3 2 1

■ ■ ■ Acknowledgments ■ ■ ■

To my companion Elder Hirschi, who brilliantly demonstrated the 8-Step Door Approach for me, and whose boldness as a missionary I have yet to meet his match.

To my companion Elder Lee, who fed and took care of me like only a mother could, and who was in my estimation the best missionary teacher I have ever seen.

To my mission president, Ed Jolly Pinegar, whose belief and confidence in me raised me to levels of performance I did not think possible, and for teaching me to love the Book of Mormon and the Prophet Joseph Smith.

To my brother Sean, whose editing and suggestions have been superb, and who encouraged me to finish this book.

To my sister Catherine Sagers, for her stories and unique perspective that enhanced and enriched the core messages in this book.

To my father, Stephen R. Covey, who gave me the concept of a highly effective missionary and who showed the way by his example.

To my son Jacob, currently serving in the Australia Adelaide Mission, for his fresh perspective and wisdom far beyond his twenty years.

To my son David Westley, who has been my most faithful assistant on this project and for his chapter topic recommendations, helpful edits, and amazing missionary stories.

To Catherine Christensen and Emily Chambers at Cedar Fort for their thoughtful suggestions and edits and for being so responsive and wonderful to work with in publishing this book.

To my assistant, Sharlyn Hall, for her belief in me and diligent efforts in helping find a publisher.

To our family friend Brad Wilcox for his timely advice and counsel. Thank you for your frank and penetrating feedback that helped streamline my book.

And finally, to my wife, Pamelyn, who has been my greatest advocate and supporter. She modeled the approaches and concepts in this book while on her mission in Spain. Her tireless editing, suggestions, stories, and insights throughout this writing process have been invaluable. I'm grateful for the amazing missionary children she is raising, and I look forward to having her as my companion on our next mission together!

■ ■ ■ Contents ■ ■ ■

■ ■ ■ Foreword ■ ■ ■

I have had the pleasure and honor of knowing David Covey for many years as a friend and as his mission president in the England London South Mission.

David Covey is one of those wonderful missionaries who have the vision of proclaiming the gospel to every nation, kindred, tongue, and people. He paid the price of preparation. Faith was his power. Love was his motive. Obedience was his price. The Holy Spirit was his director as well as comforter; for our Savior Jesus Christ was his reason for serving. He thrills like Alma in being an instrument in the hand of the Lord; it is his glory and joy (see Alma 29:9–10). He feels like the sons of Mosiah concerning the worth of souls; they are precious (see Mosiah 28:3; Doctrine and Covenants 18:10–16). Like Ammon, he knew his strength was in the Lord (see Alma 26:11–12).

Elder Covey was devoted, obedient, diligent, full of faith and hope, and easily entreated as a missionary. While serving as my assistant, he led with love and service not commanding, demanding, or threatening. He was and is a true disciple of the Lord Jesus Christ (see 3 Nephi 5:13; John 13:34–35).

He has treated the primary step in bringing souls to Christ with candor and with true-life examples. They really work. I witnessed what he has written. It surely was the goodness of God that brought the increase . . . but one need remember we must do *all* in our power, not simply ask and go through the motions of missionary work. True principles applied bring results (see Doctrine and Covenants 130:19–21).

This book is dynamic. It can work for you directly or with small adaptations to your missionary service.

Ed J. Pinegar

Mission President of the England London South
Mission, 1985–1988 and
President of the Missionary Training Center in
Provo, Utah, 1988–1991

CHAPTER 1:

The Highly Effective Missionary

"Every significant breakthrough . . . is first a break with tradi- tion, with old ways of thinking, with old paradigms" (Stephen R. Covey, The 7 Habits of Highly Effective People, *page 29).*

■ ■ ■

I'll never forget my excitement. I was three months into my mis- sion and waiting to receive the news of who my second compan- ion would be when I learned I was going to become a trainer. I was stoked. This was my wish. My trainer was going home. He was tired and trunky and wanted to be with his family. I was sick of carrying him, and frankly, I was excited about getting a fresh missionary from the MTC that I could help shape and mold.

It was late August 1985 and I was working in the military bar- racks town of Aldershot, England. Our area covered four towns: Aldershot, Cove, Farnsborough, and Fleet. My trainer and I were fortunate to see some success in our first three months, having bap- tized two people—an eighteen-year-old friend of a wonderful family in the ward and a nine-year-old son of a member family that had not been baptized yet.

With my new companion, I was confident that nothing could stand in the way of us becoming Model Missionaries. Model

Missionaries in the England London South Mission (ELSM) were required to baptize four people in a given month. The new mission president, President Ed J. Pinegar, started this program soon after his arrival in July 1985. Our mission had been averaging between twenty-five and thirty baptisms a month, and this program, among many other ideas, was going to move our mission to greater heights. This was a bold move. Only a handful of companionships in our mission had ever baptized four people in a month. But I was convinced that if anyone could do it, it would be my companion and me.

I remember the surprised looks on my zone leaders' faces when we told them our companionship goal for the month of September was four baptisms. "Are you sure you want to go for four? Why don't you just go for one or two, and then if you achieve it, you can go for four in the next month?" They didn't believe we could achieve this goal. But we were determined. I had spent most of my freshman year in college preparing for my mission, completing six religion courses, reading missionary books, memorizing scriptures, and learning the lessons. I thought I knew what it took to achieve four baptisms, and with our obedience and faith, I felt that the Lord would sustain and bless us in our desire.

We worked like dogs. We kept all of the mission rules and guidelines. We prayed with faith and determination. We studied diligently. We fasted. We pleaded. We only baptized one person. We were, of course, happy with this one baptism, but we felt disappointed we had not reached our goal of four. Where had we fallen short? What had we left undone? What could we have done better? These questions and many others ran through my head at the close of the month.

We had done absolutely everything in our power to achieve the success we had desired, and yet we had fallen short. In my four short months in the mission field, I had observed this same phenomenon happening to other missionaries as well. They had worked hard, paid the price, obeyed the rules, yet they had fallen short. What made it worse was the fact that some missionaries who were known for being less obedient to mission rules and guidelines often baptized more than those who were diligent. Why? This is a question nearly every missionary asks him- or herself at some point during his or her mission. I was now asking it myself. What I discovered was a fascinating insight.

My mission president called it "being obedient to the principles of baptism." Besides being personally righteous and obedient to the mission rules, it was also important to be obedient to those principles that brought about baptisms. Some of those principles include opening your mouth, having plenty of people in your teaching pool, using the soft challenge on lesson one, the Strait-Gate Dialogue on lesson two, and the Commitment Dialogue when your investigators progress has stalled (more on this later), having lessons with members present, getting investigators to come to church, committing people to be baptized, helping investigators keep commitments, and so on.

In other words, a process needs to be followed in bringing people to Christ through baptism. It is unrealistic and unfair to expect the Lord to shortcut the process. People have agency to choose, and the Lord is not going to force anybody into His church. I learned that the law of averages applies in mission work. I learned that you couldn't expect to baptize people that never attended church. I learned that it is unrealistic to hope that you could baptize four people in a given month when your teaching pool consisted of three people. I learned that the Lord is willing to do His part, but being obedient to baptismal principles is the part the Lord requires of us.

Most of the books I've read about missionary work, both before and after my mission, focus on the importance of being obedient. The main points of each book emphasize the traditional virtues of love, hard work, discipline, diligence, and faith. They refer to the importance of obeying the mission rules, being personally righteous, and relying constantly on the Lord. I fully support all of these principles. Every one of these virtues proves invaluable in missionary work.

However, this book has a different focus—to help you apply the principles that lead people to baptism. This book is designed to teach you the *skills* that will lead you to become a highly effective missionary. I'm defining a highly effective missionary as a missionary that reaches his or her full potential as an instrument in the hands of the Lord.

As missionaries we are called to be instruments in the Lord's hands (Mosiah 27:36). Now imagine for a moment that you are a farmer with acres of golden wheat ready to harvest. You hire two men to help you do the job. The first man goes out to the field and starts up the combine, a machine that has been specifically designed to harvest wheat in the most effective way possible. The second man goes out into the field with a pair of scissors. He plans to first snip each individual stalk down and then sort the grain by hand. Who will accomplish more?

The answer is obvious but underscores a vital point about the relationship between obedience and effectiveness. Imagine that the man with the scissors is up at the crack of dawn snipping away. He diligently works all day and is the last one to leave at night. While he is faithfully participating in the harvest, his ineffective methods ensure that he accomplishes little. Meanwhile, the man with the combine harvester wakes up late, goes out to work for an hour or so, and then calls it good for the day. Due to the effectiveness of his approach, in an hour of effort he harvests more than his partner does by slaving away all day.

So many people are ready to receive the gospel message. As the scriptures say, "the field is white, already to harvest" (Doctrine and Covenants 4:4). But an ineffective missionary is like the man trying to harvest wheat with a pair of scissors. Sure, he may be doing his best to help out, but if he were willing to change his approach, he could be accomplishing so much more.

Imagine if this missionary were to stop going through the motions and begin to develop the skills necessary to becoming a highly effective missionary. It would be like tossing away the scissors and hopping on the combine. A missionary that is both obedient and skillful is the best instrument there is in advancing the Lord's work. Skills and obedience are both required.

Obedient but ineffective missionaries often look with frustration at others who seem to be breaking rules and working less but bringing in a much larger harvest. Many grow disillusioned and conclude that being obedient doesn't matter. Nothing could be further from the truth. A disobedient and ineffective missionary will accomplish even less. What these missionaries need to do is learn how to be highly effective.

■ ■ ■

Are Skills Gimmicks?

I want to address at the outset of this book the criticism I some-times hear about skills. I've been told that skills have no place in missionary work. Somehow many people feel that when you are demonstrating skills you are being gimmicky and insincere. But that's simply not true. Being skillful as a missionary does not mean you aren't reliant upon the Lord. It does not mean that you aren't exercising faith. This book is about being obedient *and* effective. It is about being faithful *and* skillful.

When the Prophet Joseph Smith was translating the Book of Mormon, he found that he could only translate when he learned to combine prayer and work. He said that when he just prayed, it wasn't enough and when he just worked, it wasn't enough. But when he learned to do both simultaneously he succeeded in the translation. Oliver Cowdery didn't understand this principle. When Oliver was told in Doctrine and Covenants 6 that he would be able to translate, he just expected the Lord to supply the words through no effort of his own. But this was not the formula that the Lord had designated. After failing to translate, the Lord taught Oliver:

> Behold you have not understood, ye have supposed that I would have given it unto you when you took no thought but to ask me. Behold you must study it out in your mind (work) and then you must ask (pray) if it be right. And if it is right behold you will feel it burn in your bosom, therefore you will feel it is right. But if it be not right then you will have a stupor of thought and therefore you won't be able to translate what has been given to you. (Doctrine and Covenants 9:7–9)

Faith and work are both required for a missionary to be success-ful. Most missionaries are obedient. But a much smaller percent-age of missionaries are obedient and effective! Being obedient does not automatically mean you will be effective; they are two different things. A missionary can be very obedient but ineffective.

I believe greater emphasis needs to be placed on the work or the skills you demonstrate in missionary work. But because skills are often labeled as gimmicks, missionaries and mission presidents often discount them as being unimportant in missionary work. Or even worse, skills have been seen as something that should be avoided altogether. I do not believe that this is right. And I think it is one of the reasons a lot of missionaries are faithful and obedient but not highly effective and certainly not achieving significant breakthroughs.

Unfortunately, many missionaries do not achieve breakthroughs on their missions. A lot of them won't achieve this because they aren't willing to step out of their comfort zones and try new approaches and methods. Or they aren't willing to truly consecrate and dedicate themselves fully to the Lord.

I've learned through personal experience and observation that breakthroughs in missionary work often don't happen for the following reasons:

■ Missionaries are too focused on themselves, and they don't lose themselves in the work. Remember Gordon B. Hinckley father's advice to his homesick son: "Gordon, forget yourself and go to work." When President Hinckley applied his father's counsel, what he later called "his day of decision," the work started to progress.

■ Missionaries get stuck in ruts and become mired in mediocre habits. They just go through the motions. They forget the significance of their role in the Lord's work. They fail to reach their potential because they settle for less.

■ They are unwilling to be bold and innovative in their member and personal contacting approaches. Trying new approaches requires courage and faith. It requires you to fall on your face and to pick yourself back up a few times.

■ They are unwilling to be bold and innovative in their committing approaches. Helping investigators make and keep commitments is essential to their spiritual progress. Too many missionaries avoid challenging investigators because of their fear of rejection.

■ Missionaries don't focus on skills or learning new skills. Learning and applying effective contacting and committing approaches are critical for success in missionary work. Highly effective missionaries abandon approaches that don't work. They develop new approaches that do work.

Thousands of missionaries in 405 missions across the globe are demonstrating highly effective behaviors and getting results. One of them is the son of a good friend of mine who served his mission in the Netherlands and Belgium. Elder Craig served from June 2006 to June 2008. His story is composed of excerpts taken from a letter he wrote to my nephew.

I remember when I first got my call; I knew it was right as soon as I opened the letter. I just felt the Spirit saying that is where I needed to be. But the response that I got from a lot of people was, "Ah, you are going to have to work hard for your baptisms; yours is a tough mission."

While in the MTC I went to the temple and was praying about my mission and what the Lord expected of me. I wondered if I should set a goal for baptisms or not, and if it was prideful to say, "I want this many baptisms." But I really felt that I did need to set a goal and that there were a number of people that the Lord was expecting me to reach and help baptize. As I was praying, I got a very clear answer that there were 50 people that the Lord wanted me to teach and baptize. So, I wrote it down. I didn't make a big deal about it with other people, but I had that in my mind and in my prayers throughout my whole mission.

My first area was Tilburg. My companion and I had the chance to open it up; missionaries had not been there for ten years. It was incredible! We found some people, we taught some people, but nobody was progressing, nobody came to church the first three months of my mission, and we never even invited anybody to be baptized. I really felt like I wasn't reaching my full potential as a missionary, and it started to weigh down on me.

I learned that your purpose as a missionary is to baptize. You have to do it for the right reasons; but as missionaries, our job is to help people become converted to Jesus Christ so they can be baptized and enter the temple. A General Authority, Elder Paya, came to our mission and asked the question, "is your main purpose here to baptize?" It was really funny to see how hesitant the elders and sisters were to say yes. They didn't want to come across as not caring about the people and just caring about the numbers. But he was bold. He said, "Your only purpose is to baptize. You eat, drink, sleep, and dream baptism because that's the only way people will receive salvation." There are some missionaries who thought they were in Europe to serve people and be good examples, but not necessarily to baptize.

Anyone can achieve their full potential even in the most challenging situations and difficult missions. We will later revisit Elder Craig's story and discover how he became a highly effective missionary by using the approaches in this book.

My brother Sean teaches a year-long missionary preparation class in his Alpine, Utah, stake. He teaches prospective missionaries the formula for becoming a highly effective missionary. The formula is:

Obedience + Faith + Skills = A Highly Effective Missionary!

Often the missing ingredient between success and failure as a missionary is skills. By *skills* I mean consistently applying the three key personal contacting approaches, the three committing approaches, and the three keys to working with members (chapters 4–6 in this book). Missionary skills, approaches, questions, and techniques can be the difference between a highly effective missionary and a mediocre missionary.

Here is a quick summary of what you will learn in the remainder of this book:

Chapter 2: You will learn why numbers are important in missionary work and how they represent Christlike service to your fellow beings. After reading this chapter you will never think negatively about numbers again!

Chapter 3: You will learn how to effectively use numbers as a missionary and a leader (DL, ZL & AP). This chapter describes how to assess your own performance and the performance of missionaries under your stewardship. It also offers ideas and suggestions to improve results.

Chapter 4:   In this chapter you will learn how to be bold and effective with the 8-Step Door Approach. You will learn how to successfully use survey questionnaire approaches. You'll learn how to effectively use Golden Questions (GQs) in getting callbacks and appointments. And finally, you'll learn why it is so important to use the referral dialogue at the conclusion of every lesson, GQ, and contacting approach.

Chapter 5:   The Big Three! In this chapter, you'll learn why you never conclude the first lesson without asking the Soft Challenge, the Strait-Gate Dialogue on the second lesson, and the Commitment Dialogue when your progress has stopped. You'll also learn the importance of making and keeping commitments.

Chapter 6:   In this chapter, you will learn the three most important activities in member-missionary work: Lessons with a member present, MIRTHs (Member Initiated Referrals Taught in the Home), and the dialogue for getting member referrals.

Chapter 7:   In this chapter, you will learn how to utilize the power of your personality, unique skills, and aptitudes to reach people in your mission.

Chapter 8:   Closing comments and story.

Appendix: Survey Questionnaire (referenced throughout the book), Placing the Book of Mormon, and Callback Dialogue.

Question and Answer with John F. Grove, Mission President of the Montana Billings Mission. President Grove implemented the ideas and approaches in this book with amazing success. Learn how he did it.

This book is intended to support and enhance the principles contained in *Preach My Gospel*.

■ ■ ■

Chapter 1 Questions

1. Am I being obedient to the principles of baptism?

2. Does my monthly baptismal goal reflect my weekly numbers, or is it an unrealistic stretch?

3. Do I consider myself a highly effective missionary? What could I do to become more like the missionary I envisioned being while in the MTC?

4. What element of missionary work do I find most challenging?

5. What is the relationship between obedience and skills in achieving success?

6. Do I find it hard to step outside my comfort zone? When? Do I find myself mired in the same mediocre habits and patterns? How can I break the mold and be bold in trying new approaches?

■ ■ ■

CHAPTER 2:

Why Numbers Are Important in Missionary Work

"Wilford Woodruff baptized two thousand people on his mission in England in a short few months and . . . Heber C. Kimball baptized 1,800 in a few months. . . . There are hundreds of other brethren who have baptized tens and fifties and hundreds during their missions. Is it possible that each of you could develop some Wilford Woodruffs and Brigham Youngs who could baptize hundreds and thousands? Can we raise our sights?" (President Spencer W. Kimball, Mission Presidents' Seminar, June 1975).

■ ■ ■

You hear phrases all the time in missionary work. Do some of these phrases sound familiar in your mission?

- "It's the individuals that count; the numbers are not important."

- "Let's quit talking about the numbers; they're not what really matters."

- "I don't understand why we are asked to report our numbers each week."

- "Some missionaries get so caught up in the numbers that they forget why they are on a mission."

- "This mission seems like such a numbers game!"

My guess is that you will hear these phrases and many others like them throughout your mission. Unfortunately, a negative connotation is associated with numbers. Somehow we have connected numbers in missionary work with not caring about individuals and people.

I'd like to give you a new definition, a new paradigm about numbers in missionary work. Think of numbers in the way my mission president taught: numbers represent Christlike service to your fellow beings.

Can you find any fault with this statement? Think of it. Is there any difference between saying we had three baptisms last week or we baptized Claire, Marcus, and Tonya? In my mission president's mind there was no difference. Your numbers in missionary work represent the Christlike service you do on a day-to-day basis. They represent the individuals in your teaching pool, your new investigators, the people who attend church, the members who are present when you teach lessons, the number of copies of the Book of Mormon you gave to prospective investigators, and the newly baptized family that is now part of the ward. You can't separate the numbers from the individuals. In fact, the numbers *are* the individuals.

It is for this very reason that church leaders have created the "key indicators for conversion." I like how they put it in *Preach My Gospel*:

> Perhaps you have wondered which of your many duties are the most important. To be able to answer this question, you must understand your purpose and know how effective use of time can help you fulfill this purpose. Your purpose is to invite others to come unto Christ by helping them receive the restored gospel through faith in Jesus Christ and His Atonement, repentance, baptism, receiving the gift of the Holy Ghost, and enduring to the end. Key indicators have been identified by church leaders to help you focus on your purpose. . . . As you set goals and make plans, evaluate what you do in terms of how your efforts will add to the numbers of people represented in each of these key indicators. Your goal should be to have increasing numbers for every key indicator. (pp. 138–39, 146)

Can it be said any clearer? Missionaries who desire to fulfill their purpose must focus their goals and actions around the key indicators, or numbers, reported every week.

Christ, speaking through Joseph Smith in Doctrine and Covenants 18:10, stated, "The worth of souls is great in the sight of the Lord." The Savior then explains the great joy that comes to a missionary when he or she assists the Lord in bringing one of His children back to the fold. The Lord then suggests that if one is good, two, three, four, or more is even better. And why not? Wouldn't this whole world be better off if every person on the earth was a faithful member of the Lord's church? We know it would. That's what the Lord wants and that's why he has missionaries—to bring the blessings and ordinances of the gospel to all.

Ezra Taft Benson taught,

> We are commanded by God to take this gospel to all the world. That is the cause that must unite us today. Only the gospel will save the world from the calamity of its own self-destruction. Only the gospel will unite men of all races and nationalities in peace. Only the gospel will bring joy, happiness, and salvation to the human family. (*Preach My Gospel*, 2)

Given this, why do some missionaries and mission presidents think numbers are bad when they intuitively understand the joy the Lord tells us we feel in bringing souls to Christ? The reason: missionaries, mission presidents, and stake and ward leaders often *do not connect the numbers with the work of conversion.* Because they do not make the connection, they often incorrectly label numbers as getting in the way of bringing people to Christ through convert baptisms. This is the crux of the problem.

As I discovered with my companion on the fourth month of my mission, not being obedient to the principles of baptism was our shortfall. While we were doing all we could think of in our mission work, we simply did not find enough people, teach enough people, bring enough people to church, and involve enough members in the lessons. We spent nearly all our time looking for people, leaving little time to teach people. People can't progress to the waters of baptism until they are taught. We didn't yet understand the formula of what it meant to be obedient to the principles of baptism.

I am happy to report that by the end of January 1986—my eighth month out in the field—having faithfully applied this formula, my companion and I baptized four people. The next sixteen months of my mission, my companions and I were Model Missionaries *every single month*. Many months we baptized two, three, or four times more than the four baptisms required.

Was I being more personally righteous? No, I was obeying all the same mission rules as I had in the previous months. Was I working harder or praying harder? No, I continued to work and pray in the same way. Did my companion relationships make a difference? Not really, as I strove to love and work with all of my companions in the same way. So what was the difference? The difference was that I understood and was obedient to the principles of baptism. I developed skills that made me highly effective. I was teaching instead of finding. I was progressing people toward the waters of baptism instead of trying to progress my way into doors.

Let me tell you more about this formula. In the England London South Mission (ELSM), President Pinegar established some averages of what it took for companionships to achieve their baptismal goals. Here are the averages in the ELSM at the time I was serving in 1985–1987. I'm not suggesting that these should be the averages in your mission as the dynamics from mission to mission differ. I am suggesting, however, that the law of averages *does apply* in missionary work. In 1987, to baptize one person in the ELSM, the following number averages had to occur:

- 3 commitments for baptism dates

- 5 people to attend church

- 40 lessons, 10 of which taught with members present

- 15 new investigators found

- 30 total investigators in your teaching pool

Some companionships would baptize more and some less in a given month, but the averages for the whole mission held true. So if you had a goal of two baptisms in a given month, you would just have to double the above numbers. A goal of three, triple the above numbers. If you wanted to become a Model Missionary and baptize four people in a month, those kinds of numbers would have to be attained weekly.

The averages in 1987 were better than the averages in 1985 and 1986. The reason for this was our mission as a whole became better finders, teachers, committers, and more effective instruments in the Lord's hands. In the ELSM, you didn't blindly commit to four baptisms in a given month without knowing what it was going to take to accomplish this goal unlike my earlier experience. The missionaries took the law of averages seriously as they set their goals.

We found amazing consistency in accomplishing and achieving mission goals. When I arrived in the field, our mission was averaging 30 baptisms per month. The baptisms were more plentiful in Northern England. I was told that people were more hard-hearted and reserved in the South. Ironically, at the end of my mission, when the ELSM was averaging 130 baptisms a month with a high of 185 baptisms in one month, I was told that the place where more baptism occurred was in the South, not the North. Southern England, the Northern mission said, was where the field was ripe. In Northern England, apparently, most of the people had been converted in Heber C. Kimball and Wilford Woodruff's era and no one was left to baptize! This whole scale change in perception during the course of my mission amazed me.

It was interesting to see what happened in our mission when President Pinegar began teaching obedience to the principles of baptism. Some of the older missionaries refused to believe that you could have 50 people in your teaching pool or that you could teach 100 lessons a month or that you could really get the members engaged in the work. Unfortunately, some of these old-time missionaries never changed, my trainer being one of them. These missionaries didn't believe this kind of success was possible. They thought the new president had made the mission a numbers game. Unfortunately, we found that a lot of these "old paradigm" missionaries needed to go home so they could be replaced with more open, believing missionaries.

Contrast the difference of my first month compared with Elder Blake, who arrived exactly one year later than I did:

June 1985 Elder Covey's First Month	June 1986 Elder Blake's First Month
Teaching pool of three people	Teaching pool of 55 people
Knocked on hundreds of doors the first month. Only let in twice.	Got in every fourth door when time could be allocated to tracting.
Found 3 new investigators the first month	Found over 100 new investigators the first month
Taught 8 lessons the first month	Taught 250 lessons the first month
Learned how to get DAs (dinner appointments) with members	Learned how to involve members in missionary work
Hoped to baptize 1 person every 3 months	Expected to baptize 4 people every month
Mission-wide belief that England was a tough mission	Mission-wide belief that the Lord had prepared people to receive the gospel
Mission averaged 30 baptisms a month	Mission averaged 130 baptisms a month, with a high of 185

These figures are not exaggerated. I knew Elder Blake well; we came from the same hometown. I talked to Elder Blake about the differences between his first month and mine and documented these numbers while on my mission. We spent the second day of his mission working together. We found and taught seven new people. One of them was baptized a few weeks later. He, like several others, baptized over 100 people during his two years. That is 100-plus people who have begun their path to discipleship, many who entered the temple to receive their endowment and some who were married for time and all eternity. I know this can happen on your mission as you are obedient to the principles of baptism.

I would like to conclude this chapter by addressing the criticism I've sometimes heard directed at missionaries whose primary focus is on obtaining convert baptisms. I want to be clear that baptism is only the first step of many steps on the road to eternal life.

Your purpose as a missionary is stated on page 1 in *Preach My Gospel*: "Invite others to come unto Christ by helping them receive the restored gospel through faith in Jesus Christ and His Atonement, repentance, baptism, receiving the gift of the Holy Ghost, and enduring to the end."

Preach My Gospel comments further: "Your success as a missionary is measured primarily by your commitment to find, teach, baptize, and confirm people and to help them become faithful members of the Church who enjoy the presence of the Holy Ghost" (10).

So clearly the end goal is faithful members of the Church who have the privilege of making it back to our Heavenly Father's presence. Unfortunately, many people who are baptized fall away or become less active in their membership. Hence, one of the key purposes of missionary work is retention and reactivation. Missionaries will have many opportunities to help new members *stay* on the strait and narrow path after their baptism. This will be a key activity and focus throughout the duration of your mission.

■ ■ ■

Chapter 2 Questions

1. What is my attitude about missionary numbers?

2. What is my mission's collective attitude about missionary numbers? Am I positively or negatively contributing to the overall mission attitude?

3. How are missionary numbers connected to the work of conversion?

4. How are my actions as a missionary affected by the numbers?

5. How does the law of averages apply in my companionship?

6. How often do I reach my monthly baptismal goals? What do I attribute this to?

7. How am I helping recent converts and less-active members *stay* on the strait and narrow path?

■ ■ ■

CHAPTER 3:

How to Use Numbers to Increase Effectiveness

"When we deal in generalities, we shall never succeed; when we deal in specifics, we shall rarely have failure; when performance is measured, performance improves; and when performance is measured and reported, the rate of improvement accelerates" (President Thomas S. Monson, June 2004, Worldwide Leadership Broadcast).

■ ■ ■

I'll never forget my first lesson on the numbers from my mission president as a new AP nine months into my mission. President Pinegar presented several scenarios to my companion and me and then asked us to identify what problems we perceived in the companionship, not from a personal righteousness perspective but from an obedience to the principles of baptism perspective. I was amazed at how much you could learn from analyzing the numbers. Let me take you through this experience. Notice what insights you gain from looking at these scenarios.

In order to do so, it is important to share with you the definitions. In chapter 8 of *Preach My Gospel* you can find a more detailed summary of each.

Abbreviation	Definition
Bap	# of investigators Baptized during the week
Con	# of investigators Confirmed during the week
Date	# of investigators who have agreed to be baptized on a specific Date
AC	# of investigators that Attended Church that week
LMP	# of Lessons taught with a Member Present during the week
OL	# of lessons taught without a member present, Other Lessons
Prog	# of investigators that are Progressing toward baptism by keeping their commitments
RR	# of Referrals Received and have yet to be contacted
RC	# of Referrals Contacted
NI	# of New Investigators found during the week
Ret	# of lessons taught to recent converts or less-active members, Retention

In addition to the standard key indicators, in the ELSM we also reported our numbers on other key mission-wide focuses (listed below). Your mission may include additional key indicators to the ones in my mission. Each mission is different.

Abbreviation	Definition
Hours	# of Hours spent proselyting during the week
TI	Total # of Investigators in a companionship teaching pool
SQB	# of survey questionnaire blocks completed*
BOMs	# of copies of the Book of Mormon placed during the week

*One survey questionnaire block represents 12 people that answered all the questions in the survey. See Appendix for the sample survey questionnaire. I will share more about the survey contacting approach in the following chapter.

Several important points need to be mentioned before we jump into the scenarios. Lessons, new investigators found, lessons with a member present, and total investigators are all represented on an individual basis. In other words, if you find a family of five (with all five at or over the age of eight) and teach that family of five the first lesson with a member present, then the numbers in this case are represented as follows:

5 Lessons
5 Lessons with a member present
5 New Investigators
5 Total Investigators added to teaching pool

In my work and conversations with various missionaries throughout the world, I have been amazed that they would look at the above scenario with the following outcomes:

1 Lesson
1 Lesson with a member present
1 New Investigator
1 Total Investigator added

I would then ask them if this family were baptized, would the mission only count it as one baptism. They all uniformly answered, "No, we record 5 baptisms." If you record 5 baptisms, then why not 5 lessons, 5 new investigators, 5 lessons with a member present and 5 total investigators added? My point is that you must treat all the numbers as individuals. What is the difference between teaching five separate people and teaching a family of five? Nothing! In fact, what I found was our mission's way of recording numbers encouraged the finding of families, whereas the other way discouraged it because it did not reward companionships in their reports. They might as well have found one lone investigator. The numbers are the same. This does not make sense!

With that said, let's introduce the scenarios. Study the numbers and see if you can find the holes or problem areas. A lot can be gleaned from a quick glance.

■ **Scenario 1:**

Bap	Con	Date	AC	LMP	OL	Prog	RR
0	0	0	0	5	20	0	2

RC	NI	Ret	Hours	TI	SQB	BOM
2	6	4	70	30	6	12

Can you identify the gaps? The companionship is working hard, teaching lessons, finding new people, doing street contacting and door-to-door contacting, and placing copies of the Book of Mormon, but no one attended church and no investigators are progressing toward baptism. The companionship is having problems getting investigators to commit. It may be that their investigators are friends who have no intention of joining the Church, let alone committing to baptism or coming to church. Perhaps the companionship has avoided the sometimes uncomfortable moment of asking the Soft Challenge, Straight-Gate Dialogue, and Commitment Dialogue. There could be a number of things happening.

Scenario 1 Summary: Investigator Commitment Problem

■ **Scenario 2:**

Bap	Con	Date	AC	LMP	OL	Prog	RR
1	1	1	2	5	25	0	2

RC	NI	Ret	Hours	TI	SQB	BOM
2	0	3	68	26	5	12

In this scenario it is a little harder to see where the problem is. The hours are there, lessons are happening, two people attended church, a baptism occurred, and five survey blocks were completed. The one glaring statistic is *no new investigators*. The companionship is doing the survey blocks, and even placing copies of the Book of Mormon, but it is not translating into new investigators. Perhaps they could use some help with survey transition to new finds. Maybe they could get better at utilizing the Referral Dialogue (see chapter 4). Something is happening in their contacting that is not translating into new investigators.

Scenario 2 Summary: New Find/Contacting Problem

■ **Scenario 3:**

Bap	Con	Com	AC	LMP	OL	Prog	RR
0	0	2	0	8	30	4	4

RC	NI	Ret	Hours	TI	SQB	BOM
3	12	5	72	48	6	14

The numbers look good in this scenario. The hours look good, and a lot of lessons are being taught with a healthy percentage of those coming from new investigators. The companionship is working hard as evidenced by the survey blocks and Book of Mormon placements. The one glaring area is that *no one attended church*. This is especially concerning given that two investigators are committed to baptism, with four more progressing to baptism. Why would none of them attend church? This is something you can follow up on as a DL, ZL, or AP. In fact, the biggest indicator of whether a baptism happens is having investigators attend church. Investigators can't be baptized until they attend church two times (this requirement differs from mission to mission). It is as simple as that. I found in the ELSM that the Attending Church category was an even better indicator than the Progressing and Committed category. It is not surprising to see progressions and commitments fall through. Missionaries that consistently bring more people to church baptize more. Period!

Scenario 3 Summary: Attending Church Problem

■ **Scenario 4:**

Bap	Con	Com	AC	LMP	OL	Prog	RR
0	0	0	0	0	20	1	1

RC	NI	Ret	Hours	TI	SQB	BOM
0	1	0	54	68	1	22

This scenario is a little more obvious, but it has some interesting points. The low proselyting hours are concerning. The lessons taught throughout the week are not bad, but no one is progressing. Also, no lessons were taught to recent converts or less-active members. So there appears to be little or no effort in reactivating existing members. There are sixty-eight investigators in the teaching pool, no one attended church, and only one person is progressing. You would have to ask the question about how many people in the teaching pool are seriously taking the lessons. There can be the tendency in certain missions to hold on to all investigators—especially ones that enjoy having missionaries around, but have given up seriously investigating the gospel.

Another concern is the low survey questionnaire blocks. Not only is this companionship not working hard in terms of their hours, they are not working hard to find new investigators. When you see a low number in new finds, you should expect to see a strong effort resulting in many survey questionnaire blocks. This is not the case in this scenario. You also have to wonder about the Book of Mormon placements. Is the companionship simply giving away books, or are they really trying to get commitments to read with the intent to take the lessons. My wife told me that in her mission in Spain, during a period of time, her mission leadership overemphasized the placing of the Book of Mormon. This led companionships to place numerous copies of the Book of Mormon, but took focus off their mission purpose, which was to lead people to Christ through baptism. Attending church, progressing, and committing investigators are more important indicators than placing the Book of Mormon.

Scenario 4 Summary: Numerous problems

■ **Scenario 5:**

Bap	Con	Com	AC	LMP	OL	Prog	RR
2	2	3	5	20	40	4	5

RC	NI	Ret	Hours	TI	SQB	BOM
5	20	8	72	50	3	12

You're probably wondering what is wrong with these numbers? The answer is *nothing*. These are model numbers and certainly the numbers that missionaries should strive to reach each week. They represent the philosophy **progress investigators** and **find as you go**! The ELSM had a weekly standard of excellence award based on achieving balanced numbers in each of these categories. As our mission matured, the weekly standard increased. These kind of numbers achieved weekly will produce four to eight baptisms a month consistently month after month.

Scenario 5 summary: Standard of excellence numbers. No problems!

If in your mission numbers aren't a focus as I have demonstrated above, then you can certainly focus on it as a companionship. This exercise and analysis can be done individually or as a companionship.

Undeniably, if a mission wants to achieve its full potential, leadership must learn to read numbers to identify weaknesses and provide rewards for improvement. Missionaries must understand the key connection between the numbers they report with the baptisms that are realized.

■ ■ ■

Chapter 3 Questions

1. Review your key indicators as a companionship for the past month. What have been your strengths? Weaknesses? What changes could you make in your approaches that would improve areas of weaknesses? How can you support each other as a companionship?

2. As a DL, ZL, or AP, review your key indicators for the past month. What have been the strengths? Weaknesses? What changes could you make in approaches that would improve areas of weaknesses? What other resources are available to help you?

■ ■ ■

CHAPTER 4:

Contacting Approaches:

The 8-Step Door Approach, GQs,

and the Referral Dialogue

*"Nothing happens in missionary work until you find someone to teach. Talk with as many people as you can each day. It is natural to be somewhat apprehensive about talking to people, but you can pray for the faith and strength to be more bold in opening your mouth to proclaim the restored gospel" (*Preach My Gospel, *156–57).*

■ ■ ■

I mentioned my dismal door-to-door results in the first month of my mission. My companion and I literally knocked on hundreds of doors and were only let in twice. I couldn't believe that this was how missionary work was to be conducted: knocking on doors, speaking for a few seconds, and then having the door slammed in your face. As frustrating as that was, the missionaries in the ELSM at the time seemed convinced that this was the only way.

I remember thinking, *Two years of this. No wonder missionaries look forward so much to their two luxuries in life: food and sleep.* I remember asking my trainer, "Isn't there any other way?" He answered, "Not that I know of, but I'm open to any ideas you have." I didn't know of any ideas; this missionary thing was new to me. But I remember thinking, *I'm not going to continue with this approach next month.* Luckily for me, I didn't have to. Next month President Pinegar arrived with his enthusiasm, his philosophy, and—most important—his contacting approaches.

Before I go into contacting approaches, let me be the first to say that doing missionary work through members is and will continue to be the most effective way to conduct missionary work. More will be said on member work in chapter 6. However, given the reality of missionary work, you cannot rely solely on members to provide people for you to teach on your mission. You must have ways to find people through your own efforts. I will highlight the three approaches that brought me the most success in my mission. I believe these three approaches, applied diligently, can do the same for you. Note: In some missions, tracting door-to-door is not allowed. If this is the case in your mission, please apply the survey questionnaire approach in all other ways except door-to-door contacting.

■ ■ ■

1. 8-Step Door Approach

I was one month out on my mission when President Pinegar brought the survey approach to the ELSM. He said the purpose of the survey approach was threefold:

1. **To help missionaries engage potential investigators for a few minutes.** As I have indicated, the door approaches we had been using lasted only several seconds: "Hi, we're missionaries from The Church of Jesus Christ of Latter-day Saints, and we'd like to—"*SLAM.* The idea of the survey is to get the person taking the survey to open up and share his or her opinions, values, and beliefs.

2. **To get into the house or to get a return appointment.** If you were going door-to-door contacting, ideally you would take the survey inside their living room, not outside their door. If you are taking the survey on the street or on the bus, the purpose of the survey is to get a return appointment to teach a lesson.

3. **To successfully transition from survey to first lesson.** The main purpose of the survey is not for polling purposes. We aren't representatives of the Gallup organization; we are representatives of the Lord Jesus Christ. The survey must lead to a first lesson or an appointment to come back later and teach a first lesson to be considered a success.

Before going into the 8-Step Door Approach, let's look more closely at the survey questionnaire. Please stop reading at this point and go to the Appendix and look at the survey questionnaire after the Appendix page. Below the ten questions you will see the numbers one through ten and blank boxes vertically and horizontally. I refer to this as a survey block or survey questionnaire block. When you are taking the survey questionnaire at a door or on the street, you will write in the blocks yes or no. As you take the survey you go down vertically to fill in the participant's yes or no answers. You have the opportunity to survey eight people in the survey questionnaire I've included in the Appendix. Outside of question six and nine and any follow up questions you may choose to ask, all answers to the survey are a simple "yes" or a "no" answer. Your survey block might look like this after surveying three people in the street:

1	yes	yes	yes					
2	yes	no	yes					
3	yes	no	yes					
4	no	no	yes					
5	yes	yes	yes					
6	hb	hb	wog					
7	no	no	yes					
8	no	no	yes					
9	fam	fam	nature					
10	y-$	y-$	y-$					

We adjusted the questions in the survey several times during my mission. I will present the questions that seemed to work the best both for my mission and for other missions that have used the survey in their contacting approaches.

The questions are as follows:

1. Is a close, strong family important to you?

2. Should churches provide better programs for families and youth?

3. Do you have a belief in God?

4. Do you believe in Jesus Christ as the Son of God?

5. Have you ever asked yourself questions like, "Where did I come from?" "Why am I am here on earth?" and "Where will I go after I die?" Do you think that there are answers to these questions?

6. Do you believe the Bible to be the word of God or just a history book? If knew there was another book of scripture written by prophets that testifies of Christ, would you read it?

7. Do you pray?

8. If so, do you feel that God hears and answers prayers?

9. How do you cope with a crisis in your life?

10. Would you like to be happier than you are now? What would make you happier?

In administering this survey, key connections are made with each question. They will help you understand the person's background and interests.

◼ Question 1: Is a close, strong family important to you?

It is important to begin the questionnaire by focusing on families before religion or one's belief in God. If we had started off the survey with: "Do you believe in God?" we would have significantly fewer opportunities to continue with the survey. Between each question, you have an opportunity to ask a number of follow-up questions.

Follow-up questions: Do you have a family? How many children do you have?

■ **Question 2: Should churches provide better programs for families and youth?**
Here you are making the connection with families and church, which will ultimately lead to follow-up questions regarding belief in God and Christ.

Follow-up questions: Are you a churchgoer yourself? Which church do you attend?

■ **Question 3: Do you have a belief in God?**
Here you can learn about their feelings/values about God.

■ **Question 4: Do you believe in Jesus Christ as the Son of God?**
I was amazed at the number of people who believed in God but did not believe in Jesus Christ as the Son of God.

Follow-up questions: Do you believe in Jesus Christ as a prophet? A great teacher?

■ **Question 5: Have you ever asked yourself questions like, "Where did I come from?" "Why am I here on earth?" and "Where will I go after I die?" Do you think there are answers to these questions?**
I still think that these are the three best Golden Questions we have in the Church. Our understanding of the pre-earth life, the purpose for coming to earth, the spirit world, and the three degrees of glory is so comprehensive and glorious that we forget how important these questions are for people who don't have this knowledge.

■ **Question 6: Do you believe the Bible to be the word of God or just a history book? If you knew there was another book of scripture written by prophets that testifies of Christ, would you read it?**

This question generates two kinds of responses: 1) for those who believe and read the Bible, their most common response is that only the Bible is the word of God, but their curiosity about this other book of scripture is piqued, and 2) for those who don't necessarily read and believe the Bible, their curiosity is also piqued. In either case, you have set yourself up for introducing the Book of Mormon in the first lesson.

■ **Question 7: Do you pray?**

This is a great question because as a missionary you will encourage them to pray and ask God for a confirmation of the truthfulness of the message you are sharing.

■ **Question 8: If so, do you feel that God hears and answers prayers?**

This is another great question because it asks them about the efficacy of prayer in their life. A positive response to this question suggests that they can also learn for themselves the truthfulness of your message.

Follow-up questions: Can you point to an example when your prayer was answered? This can be a great confidence builder for them and a positive example for you to highlight when challenging them to ask God if Joseph Smith was a prophet or if the Book of Mormon is true.

■ **Question 9: How do you cope with a crisis in your life?**

This question helps understand their anchors in their life whether it is God, family, friends, etc.

■ **Question 10: Would you like to be happier than you are now? What would make you happier?**

This is an excellent way to close the survey because it finishes off on a lighter note. This question examines their priorities. The most common responses are "Having more money would make me happier" or "I am very satisfied with my life and there isn't anything that would make me happier" or "Who wouldn't want to happier, everybody wants to be happier than they are now."

These are just sample dialogues. Adapt everything to your own personality, mannerisms, situations, and circumstances. But always remember to

1. Praise the people when they give a positive answer. People learn three times as fast when they are praised.

2. Agree, when sincere, with them and tell them you feel just like they feel.

3. Use appropriate follow-up questions such as the following:

    ■ Yes, you care about God, then surely you want to hear about God's plan for you and your family.

    ■ Yes, you care about families, then surely you'll want to hear about how families can be together forever.

    ■ Yes, you would like to read a book written by the prophets who testify of Christ, then surely you want to read the Book of Mormon: Another Testament of Jesus Christ.

Sometimes you may get a "no" or negative response to nearly every question. But in my experience, it won't be for all ten questions. Whatever "yes" or positive response you get, you can turn into an opportunity for them to learn more.

It should be noted that in the summer of 1985 using a survey or questionnaire to contact people was not a new idea. For many years missions had used a survey approach, some with success and others with little or no success. To increase our missionaries' effectiveness and productivity, we broke down an effective approach into eight easy-to-learn steps. Mastering these steps is the key to success with the survey approach when doing door-to-door contacting.

■ ■ ■

The 8-Step Door Approach

1. Knock on the door—give a friendly greeting and smile, be enthused and excited. "Hello, sir, how are you today?"

2. Introduce yourself and your companion, shake hands, and ask for their name. There is no need to introduce the Church at this point. "My name is Elder Covey, and this is my companion Elder Lee. It's nice to meet you; what is your name?" Pause until their name is given.

3. Explain the survey—it only takes a moment. "In fact, what we are doing today, Mr. Brown, is conducting a little survey. As you can see (show them the survey), this only takes three minutes of your time. It's ten short questions concerning your opinion on a few things." "Like what?" they may ask. "Oh, just your feelings on families and other things. For instance, is a close, strong family important to you?"

4. Ask them to take the survey. "Would you be so kind as to help us for a minute?"

5. Ask to step in. "May we step in?" Moving forward. "Oh, thank you!"

6. Don't take the survey right inside the door. Ideally you need to be seated in their house. Say two magic words: "Straight through?" pointing inside their house.

7. Find a comfortable place to sit down where you can be close to them. It is also equally important that they are seated as well, or else once the survey is over, they'll be expecting you to leave. "Do you mind if we sit here? "Oh, thank you. Is there a place for you?"

8. Reaffirm the survey, give it, and move into the first lesson by asking them who they would like to have say the prayer.

> *"Oh, thank you very much for answering these questions. In fact, what*
> *we have that goes* hand in hand *(key words) with this short survey is a*
> *brief message that gives the answers to the questions where we came from,*
> *why we are here on earth, and where we are going after leaving this life.*
> *However, this message is of a* spiritual nature *(key words), so we always*
> *like to start out with a word of prayer, and since this is your home, would*
> *you like to say the prayer or would you like one of us to?"*

Without fail, they will let you say the prayer. If they are thoroughly uninterested, or if they simply don't have the time they will stop you. Otherwise you can proceed weaving in their answers and interests into the first lesson.

So, to put the eight steps into summary words:

Step 1: Smile, greet, and be enthused.
Step 2: Introduce yourself and your companion, shake hands, and get their name.
Step 3: Explain the survey.
Step 4: Ask them to take the survey.
Step 5: Ask to step in.
Step 6: Straight through.
Step 7: Sit down and have them sit down.
Step 8: "Hand in Hand" and "Spiritual Nature"

The key to the success of the door approach is *belief.* If you believe you'll get in—you will. If you don't—you won't.

As you can see, the 8-Step Door Approach is not for the faint of heart. It requires boldness, determination, and practice to be successful. It also requires that you remember your purpose as a missionary—to teach the gospel. Make no bones about it, this approach is a skill that gets better with practice and trial and error.

Several years ago, I had the opportunity to train my nephew in how the use the survey and the 8-Step Door Approach before he left on his mission to St. Louis, Missouri. Here are his words after being out in the field for six weeks:

Dear Uncle David,

I wanted to write you and thank you for sending out your book transcript. Also you will be happy to know that I started using the survey and 8-Step Door Approach two days ago. . . . So far my statistics are 9 for 18! We have gotten in 50 percent of the doors we knocked on; in every one we taught a first lesson! It is unbelievable; prior to this I had taught maybe two or three lessons a week off tracting. Last Saturday, we only tracted for three hours and taught seven lessons with six new investigators! The 8-Step Door Approach is amazing. I go to every house knowing that I am going to get in. I literally believe this will change our whole mission. The survey is amazing, how you can learn so much about the investigator and then teach accordingly. I love how you say, "May we step in?" moving forward, every time they back up and are like "uh. . . . sure." I love how you don't even ask to share a message but rather you ask, "Who would you like to say the prayer?" I just wanted to write you and let you know it is working to perfection. Thanks for teaching me the survey approach. I know the more I practice, the better it will get. Hope all is well.

Love, Elder Covey

You can imagine my excitement at receiving this letter. It has been more than two decades since my mission, and I'm happy to report that the survey questionnaire coupled with the 8-Step Door Approach still works. My nephew's story is not unique. Since the implementing of these contacting approaches in my mission, I've had the opportunity to train many missions in this approach, including the England Bristol Mission, the England London Mission, the Montana Billings Mission, the Idaho Boise Mission, the New York New York North Mission, the Massachusetts Boston Mission, the California Arcadia Mission, the Arizona Phoenix Mission, the Japan Tokyo Mission, and the Australia Brisbane Mission. I also had the opportunity to speak several times to thousands of missionaries at the MTC. The message is universally the same one. The survey questionnaire coupled with the 8-Step Door Approach has dramatically increased missionary teaching opportunities, new investigators, and as a result, more people receiving membership in the Lord's church.

Due to the candidness of the 8-Step Door Approach, new missionaries are sometimes critical of it. During my mission as a traveling and proselyting AP, I would often introduce the survey approach to new missionaries. They would cringe at the boldness required, saying that it was too "obtrusive, overbearing, and misleading." I would ask them if they thought Ammon was obtrusive, overbearing, and misleading with his approach with King Lamoni. I would say, "Okay, let's go tracting the old way, and then you can decide which approach you want to use." We would then spend an hour getting doors slammed in our faces. Once I saw a tinge of discouragement, I would then ask if they wanted to try the survey approach. Having experienced failure, they were more eager to try the approach. We would then spend the next hour teaching a first lesson after getting in one of our first four attempts with the survey. After this experience, they would begin to catch the vision of the survey.

The purpose of the questionnaire and the 8-Step Door Approach is to help a missionary facilitate why they are on their mission: *to teach*. Somehow, we have gotten that mixed up. Sometimes missionaries think their purpose is *to find*, rather than *to teach*. The survey and 8-Step Door Approach is only a mechanism that helps missionaries teach more.

Elder Ballard emphasized the importance of a teaching focus:

> I am pleased to report that with the use of *Preach My Gospel*, they (missionaries) are increasingly able to teach in their own words by the power of the Spirit and are better able to adjust their lessons to the needs of those whom they are teaching. As a result they are having meaningful impact on many lives. But quite frankly, what they need now are more people to teach. (M. Russell Ballard, "Creating a Gospel-Sharing Home," *Ensign*, May 2006)

We found in the ELSM, after a one-year implementation, that we could get in one out of four doors and teach a first discussion one out of two times for each home we got in to. This is a staggering statistic and one worth highlighting. The key to this success was boldness and strict implementation of the 8-Step Door Approach. We were fond of saying to our missionaries, "It is better to be a little overbearing than under-bearing on a mission." In other words, if you were to err on one side of the equation, you would rather err on the side of boldness.

■ ■ ■

2. Golden Questions (GQs)

Golden Questions (GQs) are thought-provoking questions you ask potential investigators in order to engage in a gospel conversation. If you don't have the opportunity to be seated in a home or on a bus, then sometimes asking single questions works better than asking the ten survey questions. Elder Ballard promised that if missionaries would talk to twenty new people every day, they would never have a shortage of investigators. But what is the best way of doing this?

Too often missionaries make the common mistake of approaching potential investigators with "Hi, we would like to share a message about . . ." Those who have tried this approach find that it rarely works. The first few moments with a contact are critical. It's the missionary's job to create an interest to learn more, and I've found that the best way to do this is by asking questions. I love the term *golden questions*, because I think the questions are just that: golden. The thought-provoking questions we ask are among the most important things we do as a missionary.

The late Truman Madsen in his lecture audiotape *Bird-Dogging* talks about the importance of asking questions. When he was a mission president, he often would ask questions as a way to start up a conversation. He tells of several key experiences in that lecture that I would like to share.

One time he was getting on a plane to attend another meeting, and he sat down next to a man who was laughing and said, "What do you know about the Mormon Church, and when are you going to join?" The man stopped laughing. President Madsen then proceeded to say, "Before you say anything, I'll have you know I'm a Mormon missionary, and I promise you if you give me any encouragement, I will talk with you from here to our destination and you will more than likely be converted." The man said, "Oh well, what the hell!" So President Madsen did talk with him the entire way. A few months later, one of the stake presidents in the area called President Madsen to let him know that this man was being baptized based on his initial bizarre encounter with some "kooky mission president" (President Madsen).

Brother Madsen relates another incident when he got in a cab and proceeded to ask the driver a number of questions about whether he was married, and if so, if he was faithful to his wife. The man responded by saying he was and that he loved his wife. At the end of his taxi ride, Truman left him with this teaser. "I want you to know that you have traveled with the only man in town who could have told you how you can live with you wife forever. Good night." The man stopped him, wanting to hear more and Truman told him about the Church and the marriage that is done in the temples for time and all eternity. The man investigated the Church and joined. He invited Truman to his wedding in the temple a year later.

Truman recounted how he talked a man who was waiting in line at the bank into investigating the Church by saying, "Are you a Mormon? You look like a Mormon." The man asked what a Mormon looked like and Truman went on to tell him how Mormons were good-looking, clean-cut, and radiated a distinguished look. He asked again, "Are you sure you're not a Mormon?" The man was intrigued enough by Truman's questions about how a Mormon looked that he investigated the Church and eventually joined. Truman finished his talk by saying that he was not anything special but that he had shown a willingness to ask people questions about the church.

The late Apostle LeGrand Richards was famous for his use of questions. He enjoyed being on planes because the people were captive and couldn't escape hearing him talk about the gospel. Elder Richards was known for his legendary missionary work. His book *A Marvelous Work & Wonder* has been instrumental in the conversion of thousands of people. Some of his famous questions are

- Do you have something better than a personal visitation of God the Father and His Son, Jesus Christ, after centuries of darkness, when the heavens had been sealed and not one religious leader believed that there was any direct communication from God upon this earth today? Do you have something better than the coming of Moroni and the knowledge of the gold plates and the marvelous message that those plates contain and that was translated by the gift and the power of God? Do you have something better than the coming of John the Baptist with the Aaronic Priesthood, the power and the authority to lead men down into the waters of baptism for the remission of their sins? Do you have something better than the coming of Peter, James, and John with the holy Melchizedek Priesthood, the power to organize again the Church and the kingdom of God upon the earth and to bestow the Holy Ghost by the laying on of hands? Do you have something better than the personal visitation of Moses, Elias, and Elijah to Joseph Smith and Oliver Cowdery in the Kirtland temple? If you know someone who has something better than that, you ought to join his church ("God's Simple Eternal Truth," BYU speech).

■ (After quoting 1 Corinthians 15:29 about baptism for the dead) "Do any of you know why that is in the Bible?" Silence. "Do any of you know of any church in the world that knows why that is in the Bible?" Silence. "Well we know all about it!"

LeGrand Richards was famous for his insightful, penetrating, and sometimes humorous use of questions as he taught the gospel.

As missionaries, we don't need to be as humorous as Elder Richards or as clever as Brother Madsen, but we do need to open our mouths. In modern-day revelation the Lord speaks to elders of the Church about the importance of opening your mouth. In the first reference, He mentions it three times.

> Open your mouths and they shall be filled, and you shall become even as Nephi of old, who journeyed from Jerusalem in the wilderness. Yea, open your mouths and spare not, and you shall be laden with sheaves upon your backs, for lo, I am with you. Yea, open your mouths and they shall be filled, saying: Repent, repent, and prepare ye the way of the Lord, and make his paths straight; for the kingdom of heaven is at hand. (Doctrine and Covenants 33:8–10)

The Lord also speaks of His displeasure with those who won't open their mouths:

> Behold, thus saith the Lord unto the elders of his church . . . But with some I am not well pleased, for they will not open their mouths,

but they hide the talent which I have given unto them, because of the fear of man. Wo unto such, for mine anger is kindled against them. And it shall come to pass, if they are not more faithful unto me, it shall be taken away, even that which they have. (Doctrine and Covenants 60:1–3)

Again, notice why some of the elders don't open their mouths—because of the fear of men. When we don't open our mouth as we go about our missionary work, we disappoint the Lord and miss out on key teaching opportunities that the Lord has placed in our path.

Here is a list of sample GQs:

- Have you heard of the Mormons?

- Have you wondered why Mormons build temples throughout the world?

- Do you believe that God speaks to prophets today as He did to prophets in the past?

- If there is a question you could ask God, what would it be?

- Have you ever heard of the Book of Mormon?

- What do you believe happens to those people who never hear of Jesus Christ? Are they damned? Or does God have a provision in place to rescue these souls?

- Have you ever wondered why there are no prophets on the earth today? What would you think if I told you that there really are prophets on the earth today?

- Do you believe that marriages and families will continue to be together after this life?

- How do you stay close to God?

- What do you do to ensure that you are living in accordance with the commandments of God?

- Any of the ten survey questions are terrific GQs to ask frequently as well.

There are a limitless number of questions you can ask. Try them out and find the set of questions that work best for you. For me, I found my best GQ questions are

1. Have you heard of the Mormons?

2. Have you ever asked yourself "Where did I come from? Why am I here on earth? And where am I going after I die?"

I found that these two GQ approaches are thought-provoking enough to get people talking. Getting people to talk is the key. These two questions are also neutral and uncontroversial. In contrast to my favorite two questions, someone may react negatively to the following question:

Question: "Do you believe that God governs our affairs?"

Answer: "Well of course not! Why would there be so much suffering in the world?" or even worse, "Why did God let my husband die?"

So I recommend avoiding questions like this and sticking to neutral and non-controversial questions. I personally baptized fifteen people on my mission from the use of GQs. I didn't use any unique or dramatic questions. In fact, the main question I used was, "Have you heard of the Mormons?" or "Do you know anything about the Mormons?" This normally gave me the opportunity to talk about Mormons and what we do as missionaries. In some cases, it led to a return appointment and in some cases to conversions from those return appointments.

With the 2012 US presidential election, where Mitt Romney was elected as the Republican party nominee (had he won, he would have been the President of the United States), the I'm a Mormon ads, and the wildly popular Broadway play "The Book of Mormon" now spreading to London and Europe, Mormons are more well known and recognized today than ever before.

The question I selected at the beginning of the 8-Step Door Approach (also used in street contacting) is not accidental. "Would you be so kind as to help us for a moment?" so as to suggest that they are not very kind if they don't help you.

I served the majority of my mission in south London. This afforded me constant opportunities to open my mouth because there were so many people everywhere I traveled. Once while Elder Hirschi and I were walking to one of our appointments, we met a Jamaican man by the name of Renald (Ron) Whiley. We asked him if he had heard of the Mormons, and he said that he had not. We told him that we were ministers of the Lord Jesus Christ and that we had come all the way from America to share a glorious message with him.

We told him that we would be back in town the following evening and asked if we could come by his house to tell him about our church and to share a message. He was intrigued enough to give us his name and his address. I don't remember anything more about the original appointment we were headed to when we found Ron, as they stopped their investigation shortly after that visit.

Ron Whiley, however, was different. He and his wife, Ivy, were deeply spiritual people who had studied the gospel and were seeking for answers to their questions. In fact, they had been investigating the Jehovah's Witnesses religion for the last three and a half years. We taught the Whileys the gospel, they embraced the Book of Mormon and the Church, and they were baptized six weeks and one day after that initial GQ on the street. In Ron's first fast and testimony meeting, he declared in his unique Jamaican voice: "I knew that when I met Elders Hirschi and Covey on Blondedale Street that I was a wanted man, wanted of the Lord. I just had no idea that there were so many wanted men and women in this church."

So there it is! There are indeed "many wanted men and women" that the Lord wants in His Church if we but learn to open our mouths and talk to the people that He has placed in our path. And we don't have to be clever or smart or have the perfect questions to ask. We just have to create enough interest to have them give us their name and address, and of course, be conveniently in the area the next evening to teach them. That shouldn't be too hard since that is what we do as missionaries.

Ron and Ivy are rocks and pillars in their ward and community. That wouldn't be happening if Elder Hirschi and I were fearful and didn't open our mouths. It is so easy to do, such an easy habit to acquire, but one that most missionaries won't do because they don't want to look awkward. But when you think about it, what is the worst that can happen? They can tell you no, go away, get lost. For the record, that happens about half the time. So what! Big deal! If the Ron and Ivy Whileys get baptized as part of the whole process, I'll take that rejection half the time.

My sister Catherine also served in the ELSM one year after I did. When my parents visited her after her mission, they reported that they had never seen such boldness in asking Golden Questions, contacting, and in getting return appointments as they saw in the ELSM. My father has trained and toured literally dozens of missions throughout the world, so we both took this as a great compliment.

After the first discouraging month of my mission, I wrote my father asking what he would recommend I do. He wrote a lot of things and offered a lot of advice, but there was one statement that stood out among all the things he said. It was, "Never let the 99 teach you about the 1!" In other words, don't let the 99 people who reject the gospel teach you about the 1 who will accept it. Unfortunately, at the time it seemed to be, "Never let the 10,000 teach you about the 1!" But this counsel really stuck with me. So many times it seems we get discouraged by those who reject us that we are not at our best with those who are ready to accept us and our message.

Let's go back to Elder Craig's story as he talks about getting outside your comfort zone, using GQs effectively, and teaching on the street.

> At the beginning of my mission it was tough to talk to everybody. But a phrase came to me one time when I was praying. It was to get outside of my comfort zone. Initially this was very difficult. I had to ask myself, Am I going to stop someone I pass while riding my bike? Am I going to stand up on a bus and talk to people? If you are always getting outside of your comfort zone, the Spirit will be your guide.
>
> Don't approach a contact saying, "Hi, we are missionaries from The Church of Jesus Christ of Latter-day-Saints." People shut down when we said that. Start off by asking a question. With immigrants, what touches their hearts is to speak their language. Learn how they greet each other in their native tongue or dialect, ask them how their country is doing, and ask them their name. This invariably opens them up to talk.

Something that I learned is to actually teach people right on the street. Set a goal to teach them a principle and commit them to do something, even praying with them on the street; it makes all the difference in the world.

■ ■ ■

3. Referral Dialogue

Finally, let's talk about the Referral Dialogue. No approach is easier, more accessible, and more successful in gaining new potential investigators than the Referral Dialogue. What is the Referral Dialogue? Simply put: "Do you have any family members, friends, or work associates who would be interested in hearing these lessons?" This is an easy question that should be asked at the end of each lesson.

It was not uncommon to have investigators fall off after the second or third lesson, but by then they had introduced us to new people as a result of the Referral Dialogue. I remember many times being surprised by the positive responses received from investigators. One time a guy said, "Yes, I'm glad you've asked me that question. I have several friends that would be interested in hearing the lessons. Here are their names and numbers," he said handing me a piece of paper. "I've already told them you would be calling. By the way, I'm not interested in proceeding any further with the lessons myself."

As it says in *Preach My Gospel*,

> Finding and teaching are related connected activities. In all teaching situations such as finding, teaching investigators, working with members, ask, "Who do you know who would be interested in and benefit from this message?" After receiving a referral, ask, "Who else can benefit from our message?" Do not hesitate to bring this up again and again in later meetings. As those you teach experience the blessings of the gospel, their desire to share it will increase (see 1 Nephi 8:12). They will often make new friends while learning the gospel. Missionaries who apply this principle usually have many people to teach. (pp. 158–59)

Gaining referrals through this process is a great opportunity. Whether at the end of a discussion, after a refusal to take the survey, or at the end of a series of GQs, the Referral Dialogue can be used in all circumstances. It can be one of the keys to adding new investigators and it is so easy to ask. Don't ever pass up the opportunity to use the Referral Dialogue.

■ ■ ■

Chapter 4 Questions

1. Am I proficient in using the 8-Step Door Approach when I do door-to-door contacting?

2. How often do I get invited into homes when I use the survey questionnaire and the 8-Step Door Approach?

3. When traveling to and from appointments, do I take the time to ask GQs?

4. What are my three favorite GQs to ask? How effective are they? Am I getting return appointments from my GQs and street contacting?

5. Do I use the Referral Dialogue at the end of each investigator lesson?

6. Have I taught anyone this week or month as a result of using the Referral Dialogue?

■ ■ ■

CHAPTER 5:

Committing Approaches:

The Soft Challenge, the Strait-Gate

Dialogue, and the Commitment Dialogue

"After all that has been said, the greatest and most important duty is to preach the Gospel" (Joseph Smith, Teaching of the Prophet Joseph Smith, *113).*

■ ■ ■

Without question, your ability to succeed on your mission with convert baptisms will be largely determined by your ability to help your investigators make and keep commitments. The baptismal covenant is a commitment to follow the Lord Jesus Christ and His teachings. Before this commitment can be made, a series of other commitments that must be made, including the commitment to come to church and to obey the Word of Wisdom, the law of chastity, and the law of tithing. These commitments are in turn based on commitments to hear the discussions, read the Book of Mormon, and pray to know whether Joseph Smith is a prophet of God and that the Church is true. All of these commitments must precede the baptismal covenant. Without these commitments and others, the baptismal commitment is not possible.

Of all the commitments you will ask of your investigators, the **Big Three** are the most important. So what are they?

■ ■ ■

1. The Soft Challenge

The Soft Challenge is used at the end of the first lesson. It is a simple question: "If you knew these things to be true, would you be baptized?"

This is an amazingly easy question to ask but unfortunately it is not consistently used. An affirmative response to this question leads directly to other important commitments. Let me illustrate the importance of getting a Soft Challenge commitment before getting other commitments through a story that demonstrates what happens when you don't commit.

In the first week of my mission, my companion and I had the opportunity to teach a woman named Mary about the commandments, including the law of tithing. I was excited but needed to prepare pretty extensively, as the MTC focused all of our time on memorizing the earlier lessons. I asked my companion how the earlier lessons had proceeded, how Mary was doing in her earlier commitments, how she enjoyed church, and what date was set for her baptism. I was very surprised when my companion responded, "Well, we haven't yet mentioned baptism, and I don't want to mention it until we have the right moment." "The right moment?" I asked, "When do you get the right moment? Besides, aren't you supposed to mention baptism at the end of the first lesson? They taught us that in the MTC." He didn't like hearing that. Here was the new missionary telling him, the experienced missionary, how it was supposed to be done. He told me to get prepared to teach two of the principles in the lesson and to leave any discussion about baptism up to him. I reluctantly agreed.

Well, we taught the lesson on the commandments. She had a lot of questions about tithing and her ability to pay it given her financial situation. She hadn't read her reading assignment, neither had she kept her commitment to read and pray about the Book of Mormon. She seemed to be confused about why she was taking the lessons, as there was no overriding purpose for doing so. I wanted many times to talk about baptism and how that was the purpose for taking the lessons, but I had promised my companion that I would leave it to him. At the end of the lesson, my companion committed her to hear the rest of the lessons, which after some pleading on his part, she consented to do. I remember thinking, "She hasn't kept any of her commitments, there was no mention of her coming to church, and she had no idea of the purpose of the discussions; how does it make sense to teach her the rest of the lessons when there are so many other things that need to be done first?" But I was only out in the field for less than a week. What did I know?

After the lesson, my companion was looking for compliments from me for getting the commitment for another appointment. I patted him on the back and said "Nice job," but felt in my heart that there had to be a better way than what he had demonstrated. And there was. It is as simple as an invitation to be baptized at the end of the first lesson that explains the purpose of why investigators take the lessons.

During the Day of Pentecost after hearing Peter deliver a powerful speech to three thousand people, the Holy Ghost pricked their hearts. They asked Peter and the rest of the apostles, "Men and brethren, what shall we do." Peter answered, "Repent and be baptized for the remission of your sins and you shall receive the gift of the Holy Ghost" (Acts 2:37–38). There was no question what should be done when moved upon by the Spirit. The scripture states that three thousand people were added to the Church that day (Acts 2:45).

Often our investigators will judge our message by how missionaries treat each other or by how they perceive us as individuals. So when preparing to ask the Soft Challenge, make sure you have demonstrated Christlike attributes in the way you've conducted yourself, because that may be the difference between whether someone accepts or rejects your baptismal invitation. My son Jacob, currently serving in the Australia Adelaide Mission, illustrated this point perfectly in his recent letter.

> We also had our sweet-as-ever Columbian investigator come to church for the first time! He has a very busy schedule trying to save money for his kids working day and night shifts, but I always knew he could create time to come to church if he wanted it badly enough.

At our last lesson, I asked him if he would be baptized when he came to know the church was true, and he said yes! He then explained the reason he would. He never questioned whether the Book of Mormon is true. He said it is true because of the person I was. He said it with so much sincerity too. He told me that he knew that I wouldn't be as good and as kind as I am if our message was false. That meant a lot to me.

In giving the Soft Challenge, you are asking investigators to do what Peter asked the Jews to do once they received a confirmation through the Spirit of the truthfulness of the gospel. A "yes" answer to the Soft Challenge is a great opportunity for you to also get their commitment to hear the remaining three lessons. Here's an example of how you can proceed:

We appreciate your time tonight and your willingness to be baptized *if* you find out the truthfulness of these things. We know that you can. As missionaries, we tell people that the very best way to learn for themselves is to take the missionary lessons. Today, we taught you the first of four lessons. Would you be willing to listen to the remaining three lessons? When is the best time for us to come back and teach you the second lesson? Thursday! Sounds good, what is the best time for you on Thursday? Eight o'clock in the evening. We will look forward to seeing you then.

Thus with the Soft Challenge, you received two commitments:

1. A commitment to be baptized if the truthfulness of our message is manifested to them.

2. A commitment to listen to the remaining three lessons.

When you think about it, what is the worst thing an investigator can say to the Soft Challenge? The worst thing they can say is *NO!* That is the absolute worst thing. You can respond to this by saying, "You don't know right now, but *if* you did, wouldn't you want to act upon those feelings by becoming a member of the Church?" Most of the time, they respond by saying, "Well, *if* I knew, I would, but I don't know." You then say, "Right, and that is why we ask you to take these lessons to explore for yourself if these things are true. And only you can find out for yourself. But I promise you that God will give you an answer to this question, permitted you ask Him in faith and in sincerity."

I've heard two other common responses to the Soft Challenge from my experience working in missions that are predominately of the Christian faith:

A. "I've already been baptized, so why would I want to do it again?" To this you don't want to respond—though it is correct—that their baptism is invalid. The best way to answer this is by saying, "You probably were baptized when you where a baby, is that correct?" Which most of the time they will answer yes to. To which you say, "The baptism we are referring to is the baptism by immersion where you are completely immersed or dipped under the water. Have you done this?" Most the time they will answer no. Of course, you always have the exceptions, which you can respond by saying, "If you were convinced of the truthfulness of these teaching about the restoration of the gospel and of the Book of Mormon, wouldn't you act upon those feelings by becoming a member of our church through baptism?" Most of the time they answer this question is a similar way as I mentioned above, "Well, *if* I knew I would, but that is a big *if.*" To which you respond, "You're right. It is a big *if,* but one worth finding out!"

B. They answer "no" to all of your rephrasing of the question. Then you say something like this: "You mean to tell me, that if God Himself visited you and told you in person these things were true and that He wanted you to be baptized, you wouldn't do it?" To which they most often respond, "Well if God himself came down, then I would believe." You can then explain how God teaches us truth through the Holy Ghost and how you distinguish the feelings of the Holy Ghost (Galatians 5:22). If they say no to this question, then my recommendation is that you ask this final question: "Do you think there would be any value in you hearing the lessons?" If they say "no," then take them at their word and know that you did your best to influence them otherwise. If they say "yes," then proceed. I baptized one person who said "yes" to this last question, despite saying "no" to all previous questions. This last question gives them the ability to opt in or out, instead of putting that decision upon you.

■ ■ ■

2. The Strait-Gate Dialogue

When an investigator has accepted the Soft Challenge to baptism, you're still only halfway there. The next step is to set a date for a baptismal service. This really solidifies the commitment and provides motivation for the investigator to continue thinking and working toward baptism. However, many missionaries struggle with setting dates; they get cautious, scared, or fail to communicate the critical importance of baptism.

The Strait-Gate Dialogue is an easy and effective way to help the investigator understand why he or she needs baptism and to see the path forward. This dialogue is used at the end of the second lesson after you have talked about the plan of salvation. It can also be taught as a short, separate lesson of its own.

There are eight steps involved with the Strait-Gate Dialogue:

1. **Review the plan of salvation**

2. **Ask them the following two questions:**

    A. Which kingdom do you want to go to? (celestial kingdom—works every time!)

    B. What two things do you need to do to get there? (1. keep commandments and 2. baptism)

Let them think. Usually they will answer "keeping the commandments," but they are hesitant to say "baptism" even though they may think of it. If they don't think of it, or even if they do, still give them the example of the child in the mud puddle (see below). Say, "The second thing that we need is this . . . Let me give you an example."

3. Example of the child in the mud puddle:

Suppose you bought a new home and you just had new white carpet laid with your new furniture. After a hard day's work of dusting and cleaning your home, you call your son in to dinner. He has been outside playing in the rain and stomping in mud puddles. You see him on the front steps about to come into your new home and ruin your carpet. What are you going to do? (Clean him up). How? (Wash him off). Why wouldn't you let him in? (Because he'd get the house dirty).

Now, we come to earth, we are all trying to keep the commandments, but no one is perfect. We all break the commandments (Romans 3:23). When we do, it makes us unclean. Is God going to let unclean people into His kingdom? (No). Why not? (Because his kingdom is perfect; we would make it dirty). So what do we need to do? (Get cleaned off). That's right—we need to get cleaned off. How do we get cleaned off?

4. Show a picture of Jesus Christ getting baptized by John the Baptist and ask them the following four questions:

    A. What's happening here? (Jesus Christ is getting baptized)

    B. By whom? (John the Baptist)

    C. Why John the Baptist? (He had the authority)

    D. How? Sprinkled or dipped under? (Immersion)

5. That's how we get cleaned off. We need to be baptized. In order to be spiritually clean and live with God, we need to keep the commandments and be baptized.

6. Drop baptism for the moment. Read Matthew 7:13–14. As you discuss the paths, draw them out on the other side of the Strait-Gate paper (see page 57 that outlines the dates, to-dos, and status) following the proper sequence of steps. If they have kids, it's fun to let the kids draw it; they love that.

7. **Ask them the following seven questions about the scripture:**

    A. How many paths? (Two)

    B. What are the paths like? (One big one and one small one)

    C. Where do they go? (One to destruction and the other to eternal life)

    D. Which one do you want to go to? (Eternal life—works every time)

    E. How many people are on each path and why? (Broad— many; narrow—few; because it is easier not to keep the commandments)

    F. So you want to get on this path. What do you need to do? (You have to go through the gate.) Read 2 Nephi 31:17. What is the gate? (Baptism)

    G. That's right, baptism is the gate by which you enter on the strait and narrow path. What else must you do? (Repent as needed and endure to the end.)

8. Turn the paper over and have a list of all the lessons, commitments required, attending church, and a baptismal date two or three weeks out at the bottom of the list (see page 57). Check off the lessons that you have already shared with them, and then briefly discuss the remaining lessons and what they cover. Tell them that you would like them to come to church. Invite them to be baptized if they find out for themselves that the Book of Mormon is true, Joseph Smith is a prophet, and that the Church is true. At this time, set up appointments for the remaining lessons as well as the dates for church.

Remember, the most important thing you can do is to use your personality during the Strait-Gate Dialogue. Follow the dialogue and let the Spirit be your guide. Let them your investigators come to the conclusions themselves from the questions you ask, and you will find that you can direct the conversation so that they will "Strait Gate" themselves.

■ ■ ■

ENTER YE IN AT THE STRAIT GATE . . .

At this time, set up appointments for the remaining lessons as well as the dates for church.

Example of Step 6:

ENTER YE IN AT THE STRAIT GATE . . .		
Narrow is the way, which leadeth unto life, and few there be that find it. Matthew 7:13–14		
Date	**To Do**	**Status**
April 1	Lesson 1: The Message of the Restoration	Complete
April 1	Commitment: Read and pray about the Book of Mormon	In Process
April 6	Lesson 2: The Plan of Salvation	Complete
April 6	Commitment: To be baptized on April 20	In Process
April 7	Attend Church	
April 10	Lesson 3: The Gospel of Jesus Christ	Next Visit
April 13	Lesson 4: The Commandments	
April 14	Attend church	
April 15-20	Invite family and friends to baptism	
April 19	Baptism Interview	
April 20	Baptism	
April 21	Confirmation	

■ ■ ■

3. The Commitment Dialogue

Let's suppose you have an investigator who has not yet committed for baptism and has heard more than three discussions. Let's say
you have already

1. Soft Challenged them

2. Talked frequently about baptism

3. Reviewed past commitments, like reading, praying, and so on

4. Attempted to plan a "Straight Gate" date

But you find they're still unable to commit to a solid date or
reveal "hidden" concerns. This Commitment Dialogue is a heart-
to-heart talk with your investigator and should not only reveal and
resolve any remaining concerns about baptism, but also help them
commit to a firm date.

As it says in *Preach My Gospel,*

> Sometimes people's concerns are like an iceberg. Only a small por-
> tion is visible above the surface. These concerns can be complex and
> difficult to resolve. For this reason you need to follow the Spirit and
> respond in a manner best suited to the situation. Pray for the gift of
> discernment and follow your impressions. Heavenly Father knows
> the hearts and experiences of all people (the complete iceberg) and
> will help you know what is best for each person. When you help
> others resolve their concerns, first seek to understand their concerns
> by asking questions and listening. (p. 187)

Ask

Questions such as these will reveal most concerns:

■ "How do you feel when we teach you?"

■ "What would be the hardest teaching for you to live?"

■ "What good things would happen if you joined the Church?"

■ "Is there anything in the Church or its teachings that is evil or would cause a person to be bad?"

■ "Is there any reason why you shouldn't join the Church?"

Listen

Learning to listen empathetically is critical to resolving concerns. As missionaries, we often need to talk less and listen more. Sometimes we are so intent to share our message, our stories, and our examples that we forget that our investigators may not be listening to us because of a concern they have or a question that they need to ask. The commitment dialogue is a reminder for us to step back and get in touch with our investigators' feelings and impressions. We can't do this while we are talking. Often it is like peeling an onion back layer by layer to get to the core issues or concerns of our investigators. It is a slow, methodical, and often emotional process.

Elder Jeffrey R. Holland taught,

> More important than speaking is listening. These people are not lifeless objects disguised as a baptismal statistic. They are children of God, our brothers and sisters, and they need what we have. Be genuine. Reach out sincerely. Ask these friends what matters most to them. What do they cherish, and what do they hold dear? And then listen. If the setting is right, you might ask what their fears are, what they yearn for, or what they feel is missing in their lives. I promise you that something in what they say will always highlight a truth of the gospel about which you can bear testimony and about which you can then offer more. . . If we listen with love, we won't need to wonder what to say. It will be given to us—by the Spirit and by our friends. (*Preach My Gospel*, p. 185)

Bear your testimony!

We know the Church is true and want you to be happy with this knowledge. Here are some things you can do to help you know for yourself:

- Study

- Pray

- Attend Church

- Let a Member Visit You

The three main things that get investigators baptized according to Ed J. Pinegar's research while MTC President in Provo, Utah, are

1. Reading the Book of Mormon

2. Praying

3. Attending Church

From my experience, more often than not, investigators don't doubt the truthfulness of the gospel or the Restoration as much as they doubt themselves. Past religious experiences may lead them to create false expectations of the preparation time necessary and where they need to be spiritually in order to be baptized. Some see it as the end of the gospel path rather than the beginning. Clearly explain that the baptismal covenant requires

1. A desire to repent and come unto Christ

2. A promise to obey the commandments as best as you can

3. A beginning testimony of the truthfulness of the Church and its teachings

If you feel like they meet these conditions, you can say, "Since you have these feelings and knowledge, will you be baptized on _____?"

These questions should bring out concerns and give you an opportunity to resolve them. Be sure to let your investigators state all their concerns before trying to address them right off, as the first concern is not always the real one. Practice this dialogue well enough to give it with your own words, in the spirit of genuine love and understanding, all the while building up and praising all their good progress.

The Big Three are key in helping investigators make and keep commitments. Missionaries that consistently apply the use of these dialogues will find that they are able to progress investigators who are ready to receive the gospel and weed out those who are not prepared.

Chapter 5 Questions

1.   Do I consistently ask the Soft Challenge after the first lesson?

2.   How often do investigators accept my Soft Challenge? Role-play with your companion and have them evaluate you. Are you hesitant? Unclear? Too overbearing?

3.   Do I take my investigator through the Strait-Gate Dialogue after the second lesson? Do my investigators feel the need and desire to be baptized? Role-play with your companion and have them evaluate you. Are you smooth and clear in going through all the steps?

4.   How often do investigators accept my Strait-Gate Challenge? When I'm not successful, do I know why? What will I do differently the next time?

5.   Do I use the Commitment Dialogue when my investigators' progress has stalled or stopped?

6.   How often do investigators accept my Commitment Dialogue challenge? Do I listen with empathy and compassion? Do I understand my investigators' concerns? Do I successfully resolve their concerns? Do I exhibit Christlike charity?

■ ■ ■

CHAPTER 6:

Three Keys to Working with Members:

Lessons with a Member Present, MIRTH (Member-Initiated Referral Taught in the Home), and Dialogue for Getting Member Referrals

---

Now, we are a busy people; but the Lord did not say, 'If it is convenient for you, would you consider preaching the gospel.' He has said, 'Let every man learn his duty,' (Doctrine and Covenants 107:99) and, 'Behold. . . . It becometh every man who hath been warned to warn his neighbor' (Doctrine and Covenants 88:81). We must come to think of our obligation rather than our convenience. The time, I think, is here when sacrifice must become an even more important element in the church. I feel the Lord has placed, in a very natural way within our circles of friends and acquaintances, many persons who are ready to enter into his church. We ask that you prayerfully identify those persons and then ask the Lord's assistance in helping you introduce them to the gospel"(President Spencer W. Kimball, Ensign, *February, 1983, 3).*

■ ■ ■

Doing missionary work with members is challenging but worthwhile. Investigators brought into the Church through member assistance are much more likely to remain active in the gospel throughout their lives compared to members found through other approaches. This certainly proved true in my mission.

Members can do a lot to assist in the work: set a good example, place a Book of Mormon with a friend, pray for the missionaries, feed the missionaries, and share their testimonies in fast and testimony meeting. But in my opinion and experience, the three most productive things members can do to hasten the work are participating in lessons, providing a MIRTH opportunity, and giving the missionaries referrals. Let's explore each of these.

■ ■ ■

1. Lessons with a Member Present

In the Book of Mormon, we find a great example of involving members in the story of one of the best missionaries of all time—Alma. Alma was called to teach the people of Ammonihah, but from the beginning he didn't stand a chance. They "hardened their hearts" (Alma 8:11) and "withstood all his words, and reviled him, and spit upon him, and caused that he should be cast out of their city" (Alma 8:13). It would be hard to find a worse reception of his message. You can imagine how he must have felt. Now this rejection wasn't due to any lack of effort on the part of Alma, for he had "labored much in the spirit, wrestling with God in mighty prayer." Even so, he had been utterly rejected. But the Lord hadn't given up on those people. He guided Alma to Amulek.

We don't know a lot about Amulek's background, except for what he tells us: "I have seen much of [God's] mysteries and his marvelous power" (Alma 10:3), "Nevertheless I did harden my heart, for I was called many times and I would not hear; therefore I knew concerning these things, yet I would not know" (Alma 10:4). It is probable that he was a less-active member, someone who had once had a testimony but had fallen away. Strengthening him and his family first, "Alma tarried many days with Amulek before he began to preach unto the people" (Alma 8:27). As Amulek later says of the time, "he hath blessed mine house, he hath blessed me, and my women, and my children, and my father and my kinsfolk; yea, even all my kindred hath he blessed" (Alma 10:10). Alma, the missionary, then takes Amulek, the member, to go teach with him (Alma 8:29).

Alma starts to teach, but once again is met with scorn. "They began to contend" (Alma 9:1) and mockingly challenge him: "Who art thou?" (Alma 9:2), "Who is God, that sendeth no more authority than one man among this people?" (Alma 9:6). Alma, not one to be discouraged, boldly preaches of Christ and calls them to repentance but at the end of it all, "the people were wroth with [him]" (Alma 9:31). Alma seems headed toward a repeat of his earlier rejection.

But then Amulek steps in. Amulek is no stranger to these people. As he says, "I am also a man of no small reputation among all those who know me; yea and behold I have many kindreds and friends, and I have also acquired much riches by the hand of my industry." He is one of them, a respectable pillar of the community. He supports Alma's message, declaring, "I know that the things whereof he hath testified are true" (Alma 10:10). "The people began to be astonished, seeing there was more than one witness" (Alma 10:11). But Amulek was not just any witness, he was their friend and their neighbor, a man who understood their way of life. His testimony astonishes them.

Meanwhile, Alma is listening as Amulek speaks. After Amulek finishes sharing his testimony, Alma "begins to . . . establish the words of Amulek and to explain things beyond, or to unfold the scriptures beyond that which Amulek had done" (Alma 12:1). He clarifies what Amulek has taught, and continues to direct the lesson. There is teamwork between member and missionary. The result is wholly different from Alma's first time around. "And it came to pass after he had made an end of speaking unto the people many of them did believe on his words and began to repent and to search the scriptures" (Alma 14:1).

The power of testimony is great. The power of several witnesses is better than the power of one. Nothing is more powerful in the world than having a member bear testimony of the gospel in a lesson. The investigators expect the missionaries to bear testimony. When a local member also bears testimony, a more powerful impression is created than by the missionaries alone. The member is seen as someone who is more objective, who holds a job (in other words doesn't do missionary work for a living), and is very much like the investigator. The member may have been in the investigator's shoes. This builds enormous credibility and realism in the lessons.

When a missionary teaches lessons with a member present, the investigator has an instant network into the Church. Missionaries come and go and are not long-term players in the area. Members, on the other hand, are stable and consistent. There is not a better feeling than to have a member say hello to an investigator at church after they have met them earlier in a lesson; or, even better, to have a member invite an investigator to a church activity without the missionaries even knowing.

Lessons with members present are also great for members. Members have a hard time knowing how they can best participate in missionary work. Inviting a member to sit in on a lesson and bear their testimony is relatively easy for them to do. They don't need to prepare anything, have any fears of rejection, or feel guilty for not talking with their friends about the church. It is simply the best way to instantly get them involved in the work. Members catch the missionary vision by being part of a lesson more than almost any other activity. I invite all missionaries to take advantage of the power that comes from lessons with members present. In the ELSM we saw incredible results only when we seriously involved members in missionary lessons.

■ ■ ■

2. Member-Initiated Referral Taught in the Home (MIRTH)

Of course, we couldn't talk about missionary work without talking about member referrals. The most successful member referrals are a Member-Initiated Referral Taught in the Home (MIRTH). During my mission when my companion and I received a MIRTH, it resulted in a baptism more than half the time.

Let me illustrate. In my second area, I was assigned to the lovely southern coastal city of Brighton. Brighton is fifty miles directly south of London. It is a beautiful city with abundant beachfront property. Every summer, you see a flock of white bodies out on the beach trying to soak up the rays at Brighton.

One of the first things we did was to take the outdated ward list and follow up with less-active members and part-member families. It was early December 1985 when we visited the less-active Bridle family, consisting of Janice Bridle and her three children, Claire, Marcus, and Tonya, ages fifteen, thirteen, and twelve. This was a family that was golden in every possible way. We taught them the lessons and were able to reactivate Janice and baptize her three children. I was only in Brighton for four months, but my sister Catherine served in Brighton three years later and reported to me that the Bridle family had been instrumental in bringing in thirty to forty new members to the Brighton ward since their baptism. The weekly sacrament attendance was only sixty to seventy people at the time the Bridle children were baptized. Three years later, when my sister was there, a new chapel was built to accommodate all the people coming to church. The majority of the new converts were coming because of their association with the Bridle family, who were willing to have all the lessons taught by the missionaries in their home. What a difference helpful members can make!

Elder Craig shares some stories of working with members:

> I was transferred to another area—a bigger city named Rotterdam—and there I started seeing more success in people being baptized. Something that I learned in Rotterdam is the importance of working through members.
>
> There was a single mom with two teenage kids who loved missionary work. We had at least one investigator, and sometimes up to five, every week at her home for the six months that I was there. Every single one of them was baptized. We typically did our teaching on Thursday nights. It was a hassle getting to her home because we had to take a very long bus ride. But once we had arrived, we felt the Spirit, and there is nothing that can replace the Spirit in the home of a member. This good sister brought many people into the Church.
>
> Eventually you want to get members to invite their own friends, but as you bring people into their homes and help them see you can teach and bring the Spirit, they get really excited about the work. It's a step-by-step process; they might not be inviting their friends right away, but you can start by asking them if you can bring investigators to their homes.

Family Mission Plans

Something that I learned later on my mission while working with members is to make family mission plans. It talks about it in Chapter 13 of *Preach My Gospel*. So my companions and I selected three families in the ward and made family mission plans with them that we creatively adapted to their own circumstances.

For example, there was Brother Familiecoat, a twenty-nine-year-old Dutchman with a young family that were huge *Lord of the Rings* fans. He used to tell his little girl *Lord of the Rings* stories before she went to bed. His wife was the Relief Society President. He was going to church but wasn't very engaged in missionary work.

His wife was a little worried about it. My companion and I decided that we were going to make a Lord of the Rings family mission plan with them. So we got a piece of paper, folded it up, wrapped it around, and glued it so it made a ring. We wrote "Familiecoat Family Mission Plan." We went into their home and began to read from Mosiah 18 about the importance of being one, and having unity with the members and missionary work.

It was going along okay, they were giving good answers, but still not too excited yet, so then we started humming the Lord of the Rings song. We pulled out the "One Ring," and we gave it to Brother Familiecoat. He got so excited and said, "Ohhhhhhh, this is amazing," and he started making all kinds of connections between the ring and the gospel. We talked about connecting to have a plan and how to make missionary goals.

The idea of these family mission plans is that each family is at a different level of missionary work, and if they make their own mission plans with goals, then they are going to be accomplishing what the Lord wants them to. They will be able to make progress instead of us missionaries coming in and saying, "Okay, here's what we want you to do to help us." Instead, you go in there with the attitude of "We want to help you do your missionary work, so let's make a plan and let us know what we can do to help." For example, have the missionaries over with investigators once a week, invite a friend to church, give away a Book of Mormon, whatever they want to do.

We did another approach with a family of five who had a twelve-year-old son that loves basketball, so we did a little basketball game with him. We took a piece of paper and designated a center, power forward, shooting guard, point guard, etc., that included each member of the family. They each had a special assignment to do in their family game plan. The twelve-year-old boy really understood it.

He made the relation to missionary work and basketball practice. It was incredible to see their enthusiasm and results when you make it personal for the family. When you show them you really care about them and are creative, they respond. They get excited about missionary work.

Missionary work is addicting once ward members start experiencing it. They start telling other members their experiences. It's amazing how much members talk to each other. They say, "Oh, the missionaries came over and they had investigators, it was amazing." You will find other members begin asking you to invite investigators over. It's wonderful.

This is the impact a MIRTH can have once a member family catches the vision. While on my mission I noticed that in every ward that I served, there were a few families that were on fire about missionary work. I mentioned the Bridle family earlier and how they were instrumental in bringing dozens of new converts into the Church. Not all of these people had started out as their friends; often they were other contacts the missionaries brought into their home that were fellowshipped and nurtured by the Bridles.

When I got to my third area, my companion and I started to prayerfully select three families in the ward to work extensively with. These were families that were ready to have missionary lessons conducted in their home, gave referrals, and could be counted on to provide fellowship and support for investigators. This didn't mean we ignored other ward members. It just meant that we had three families that we worked more closely with. We found that the Lord always had two or three families who had been prepared to really propel the work forward. It was a natural and beneficial relationship. As missionaries we felt drawn to them, and they as members felt drawn to us.

My recommendation is to prayerfully seek out two or three families in the ward you are serving to provide you with MIRTH opportunities. You can ask all members to assist in lessons, but it is helpful to focus on a few families to play a special role in providing MIRTHs.

I first learned this practice from my father. He told me the story of Elder Finlayson, who served in a California mission, that best demonstrated member-missionary work. Elder Finlayson and his companion wanted to spend all their time teaching the gospel, not finding people to teach. They shared their vision with the Relief Society President (one of their key contacts) and got her buy-in and commitment for the Relief Society sisters to provide people for the missionaries to teach. The elders rented a room in the city where they resided. The plan was for the Relief Society to organize appointments so that Elder Finlayson and his companion could teach all day long.

The Relief Society had a waiting room where investigators would show up prior to their appointment with the elders. There were magazines such as the *Ensign* and *New Era* that people could browse through while they were waiting for their appointed teaching time. The environment was perfectly conducive for them to have a spiritual experience.

Meanwhile, Elder Finlayson and his companion would spend the whole day teaching the gospel to interested investigators. They ended up baptizing dozens and dozens of people without ever having to spend time finding people. The Relief Society sisters took care of that. Wouldn't it be incredible if this approach were the standard operating procedure in all the wards throughout the world? Just think of it. Eighty thousand missionaries spending every waking moment of their mission teaching investigators twelve hours a day.

■ ■ ■

3. Dialogue for getting member referrals

I have seen many different approaches for getting member referrals. None is more effective than the dialogue my son David learned from his stake president while on his mission. Here's the dialogue:

> As a missionary you're always told that the key to success is working with the members. This is absolutely true. But I remember how frustrating it was sometimes. We would visit a family and teach a spiritual lesson. Everything would be going great, and then the dreaded question: "Do you know anyone who we could teach?" You get the same answer 99 percent of the time: "Um. . . . you know. . . . I don't really know anyone right now, but I'll be looking for opportunities.

I remember that some missionaries would get so frustrated with the merry-go-round that they would give up working with members. "The members don't want to help in this area," they would say. "I'll just wait until transfers."

As a missionary it's not your job to blame, criticize, or pressure members to help with in missionary work. They know missionary work is important. They've heard all the talks. They don't need more guilt. They need someone to make it easier for them. That's where you come in.

President Chavez, one of my stake presidents in Tegucigalpa, taught this dialogue for referrals to me. As a missionary he used it with great success in his mission in Guatemala. One time he went to do splits in an area where the work had been struggling. His companion was an elder who had been in the area for four months and couldn't wait to get out. He hadn't had any baptisms and was openly negative about the members. "They don't care about missionary work. No matter what we do, they never will give us a referral. I've been here for four months, and I know how they are." Elder Chavez took this as a challenge. Using this method throughout the day, they got over thirty solid referrals. As they left the last house, having received seven referrals from them alone, the doubting elder burst into tears. He couldn't believe it.

If you've ever struggled to get referrals from members, this might be worth trying out. Here's the process. Your first task is to set the tone. You want them to feel the Spirit and remind themselves of the importance of missionary work. There are a lot of ways to do this. I liked to ask them about their background with the Church. If they weren't first generation converts, who was? Their parents? Grandparents? Where did it all begin? I would help them see that they were in the church because someone did some missionary work. What blessings had they received as members? Why was it important to them to be members? What would they be missing if they weren't? Questions like these are great because it gets them talking; it's always better to hear yourself say, "I'm grateful for . . ." rather than hearing "You should be grateful for . . ."

To help set the tone, you can also share a scripture. I loved to share the classic, Doctrine and Covenants 18:10–18, because verse 18 ties in nicely with a later part of this method. There are many scriptures that can apply, so it doesn't really matter which you use as long as it communicates the value of missionary work.

You can also watch a movie. There's a great one in Spanish called

Por Cosas Pequenas y Sencillas (*By Small and Simple Things*) that has interviews with recent converts talking about how they joined. Your family's own conversion story and other personal experiences are always powerful. Teaching the Principles of the Restoration, lesson 1, is also great. President Chavez liked to teach about the priesthood and the necessity of being baptized by the proper authority to enter the kingdom of God. Whatever works for you. As I mentioned, it doesn't matter how you go about setting the tone; it just matters that you do so, without taking up too much time. This part should not take more than 15 minutes

Once they are in the missionary mind-set, you pull out a piece of paper for everyone in the family, including small children. Make sure to get everyone involved. Explain that you're going to play a game. Ask the family how many of their neighbors are not members of the Church. Then how many classmates. Work associates. Family members. The guy at the local café. Keep mentioning other types of people to get their brains going. Tell them that you and your companion are going to sing a hymn, and while you sing, they are going to see who can write down the most names of people that are not members. As soon as the singing stops, time is up and they can't write anymore.

Before you begin, assure them that this isn't a trap in which they have to give a referral for every name they write down, or else they may limit themselves. It's very important that they engage. Try to make it fun, ask them who they think is going to win; make it a little competitive. This works especially well with kids. I've had times where they write down as many as eighty names.

This method is far superior to the blunt question, "Do you have any referrals?" because it gives them time to brainstorm about all the people they know instead of putting them on the spot. It allows the Spirit to touch their minds and reveal who is ready to receive the gospel. Many times you'll see them having an "aha" moment as they remember someone they could talk to. They'll often surprise themselves by how many people they know.

I love what it says in *Preach My Gospel*: "You are surrounded by people. You pass them on the street, visit them in their homes, and travel among them. All of them are children of God, your brothers and sisters. God loves them just as He loves you. Many of these people are searching for purpose in life. They are concerned for their families. They need the sense of belonging that comes from the knowledge that they are children of God, members of His eternal family. They want "peace in this world, and eternal life in the world to come" (Doctrine and Covenants 59:23), but they are "kept from the truth because they know not where to find it" (Doctrine and Covenants 123:12)" (*Preach My Gospel*, 1).

Try to pick the most spiritual, beautiful hymn possible. "Our Savior's Love" is preferable to "The Battle Hymn of the Republic," as you really want to bring the Spirit into this part.

When you finish singing, tell everyone to put their pencils down. Give time for everyone to compare, see who "won" if you turned it into a competition. Then explain that all of these people that they know might not be ready to receive the gospel. Most probably aren't. But there are a few that have been prepared and have been placed in your path so that you can help them. But how can we know which ones are ready and which ones aren't?

We can't always discern very accurately, but someone can and that is God. He can reveal this knowledge to us through the Spirit, speaking to our mind and our heart (Doctrine and Covenants 8:2). Ask them if they have faith that God can do this. Then ask a family member, preferably the head of the household, to offer a kneeling prayer to ask for guidance.

This will often be a very spiritual moment. After the prayer it's okay to linger on your knees for a second. Then ask family members to look at the list of names that they had made and seek inspiration to know who is ready. Tell them to put a star next to these names. It could be one name or five.

Then have each member of the family share the names that they felt prompted to mark. Having received a spiritual impression they will feel strongly about doing something to share the gospel with them. Help them know what they can do. It's usually great to plan a MIRTH family night, in which they can be casually introduced to the missionaries. Individual plans can also be made. If the eldest daughter felt strongly about her friend Kate, she can set a goal to give her a copy of the *New Era* or a Book of Mormon. If she's nervous you can coach her and practice how to do so, though usually in a future lesson, as you don't want to drag this out too long. It's important not to get bogged down in this part as you don't want to lose the Spirit. But make sure to set a few clear, actionable commitments of what the members will do before you leave the home.

The next step is the most important. Follow up. Without follow-up it is very unlikely that they will get much done. Sharing the gospel is important to nearly all members; it's just not always pressing. They have many other things that take their attention, so it's your job to keep reminding them how important missionary work is. Make it seem pressing. And then treat the references you receive as gold. Make sure to hang on to the lists of names that they created. After you have taught the people that they felt prompted to work with as the most ready, you can branch into the other names on the list. This can be a treasure trove of future investigators.

In short, the method for receiving referrals is . . .

1. Set the tone
2. Hand out papers, explain game
3. Sing hymn while they write
4. Seek guidance through prayer
5. Identify names
6. Make plans
7. Follow up, follow up, follow up

■ ■ ■

Chapter 6 Questions

1. Do I try to teach at least one-third of my lessons with a member present? How often is it happening now? What can I do to encourage more members to participate in the lessons?

2. Have I prayerfully identified two or three families in my ward that could provide a MIRTH appointment? When do I plan to visit with them? How will I ask them for a MIRTH appointment? Role-play with your companion.

3. How many MIRTH appointments did I receive last month? What is my goal for next month?

4. Have I prayerfully identified two or three families in my ward that could provide a member referral? When do I plan to visit with them? How will I ask them for a member referral? Role-play with your companion.

5. How many member referrals did I receive last month? What is my goal for next month?

6. For investigators found through a MIRTH appointment or member referral, how many are progressing? How many have been baptized? How does this compare to investigators found through personal contacting approaches?

CHAPTER 7:

Let Your Personality Shine Forth

"The missionary should feel free to use his own words as prompted by the Spirit. He should not give a memorized recitation, but speak from the heart in his own terms. He may depart from the order of the lessons, giving that which he is inspired to do, according to the interest and needs of the investigator" (Statement on Missionary Work, First Presidency letter, December 11, 2002, Preach My Gospel, 30).

■ ■ ■

One of the themes in this book has been the importance of using your personality, unique gifts, and aptitudes to attract people to the Church and our message. No one wants to belong to an overly serious and stiff church. Missionaries are representatives of the Lord Jesus Christ, but they are also a collage of differing personalities that make life more interesting and intriguing.

I have always been so impressed with the ease that President Gordon B. Hinckley made nonmembers and the press feel around the church. He was so inclusive, non-judgmental, and clear and concise in the ways he explained our doctrine and teachings. He truly was one of God's instruments in helping the Church come *"out of darkness and out of obscurity"* (Doctrine and Covenants 1:30). Think of how many nonmembers came away favorably impressed (and some converted to the faith) because of their contact and association with President Hinckley.

President Hinckley was a man who had a great sense of humor. He was witty, natural, and fun. His personality was able to shine forth for the whole world to see. Likewise, I think it is important for missionaries to let their personalities shine forth. Too many times missionaries become entrenched in the seriousness of their work to where their personalities become muted or hidden. Now I'm not suggesting that missionaries should be frivolous and irreverent. Far from it! I am suggesting that missionaries can learn from the good example of President Hinckley and the proper balance he showed of being serious and solemn but also witty and humorous.

Like President Hinckley, the Prophet Joseph Smith also exhibited the characteristics of balance and perspective worthy of emulation by today's missionary. Joseph could be reverent and serious on the one hand and jovial, cheerful, lighthearted, and fun on the other. It is important to note that nowhere in the scriptures is lightheartedness condemned. The same can't be said of light-mindedness. Joseph did not wish to be seen as being better than other people. He believed that "a prophet is a prophet only when he is acting as such" (Truman Madsen, *Joseph Smith the Prophet*, 27). Others felt Joseph should act like a prophet all the time. New converts observed that Hyrum, his older brother, *"seemed more in the image of what they thought a prophet should look like and behave like. The Prophet, for all his sobriety under proper circumstances, was a hail-fellow-well-met, easily inclined to laughter, sociable, animated, the life of the party, and colorful in his use of language"* (Truman Madsen, *Joseph Smith the Prophet*, 25). No one, friend or foe, could ever accused the Prophet of not letting his personality shine forth.

On my mission I had plenty of opportunities to let my personality shine forth. When I was in my second area, on the lovely coast of Brighton, England, I met a young man named Stephen Bills. Stephen was very shy and had been through several dozen missionaries as an eternal investigator over the past four years. He attended church and seemed to understand all the doctrines of the gospel. I remember wondering why this guy wasn't a member of the Church.

After my companion and I met with Stephen and got to know

him better, it became apparent to us that the reason why Stephen hadn't joined the Church was because the previous elders and ward members weren't interested in Stephen Bills. They were just interested in baptizing him. And Stephen did not want to feel like a baptismal statistic.

I learned early on in my mission that nothing is more important than to follow the promptings of the Holy Ghost. Sometimes it will guide you off the beaten path, seemingly going against your training and instincts of what you think you should be doing. Such was the case with Stephen Bills. There was a reason he had gone through twelve different companionships. We didn't want to be the thirteenth companionship that was unable to positively influence Stephen toward becoming a member of Christ's church. We had to do something different than what other missionaries had done before us.

My companion and I felt impressed that we needed to learn more about him and his interests. At first he was painfully shy, and he had a hard time opening up to us. When he finally realized that we were genuinely interested in him, he started to share a few things. One of these was his love for the Beatles. I couldn't believe it. I didn't think there was another individual on the planet that loved the Beatles as much as I did. Boy, was I wrong!

Stephen knew everything about the Beatles—their songs, their stories, and the crazy things they did. He was impressed that I knew so much about them. Stephen also played the guitar and was a good singer. Who would have guessed? The three of us sang Beatles songs as Stephen strummed his guitar, trying his best to drown out our off-pitch voices.

For three straight visits we felt impressed by the Holy Ghost that we should not try to pressure Stephen about getting baptized or about the Church (truly against our natural missionary instincts and the missionary plan in this book) but felt that we should just be with him and listen to him. We ended up singing Beatles songs for the whole hour.

On our fourth visit, Stephen told us that he was ready to get baptized. He said that we were the first missionaries that took an interest in him and didn't try to pressure him to get baptized. He said that as long as missionaries tried to focus on his baptism, he would further dig in his heels and resist their attempts. He had gone through twelve missionary companionships over a four-year period and every companionship would do the same thing and ask the same questions. It became predictable to him.

I have no doubt that God used my interest and love of the Beatles to bring Stephen Bills into His church. We could have followed the letter of the missionary law and ignored the strong impressions we felt and tried to teach him a lesson or ask him probing questions. After all, that is why we go on missions! But God prompted us to use our personality to reach Stephen. Stephen has since gone to become a bishop in the Brighton Ward and has made a big contribution to God's work.

In my first area I was fortunate to follow a very successful missionary companionship. Elders Bateman and Chipman had baptized nearly a dozen people during their time in Aldershot, including the Bishop family. The mother, Vera Bishop, had been baptized and so had two of her daughters. But she also had a son who hadn't taken much interest in hearing the discussions or getting baptized. When my trainer and I arrived in Aldershot (Elder Bateman had completed his mission, and Elder Chipman had been transferred to a different area), we were told in the area book not to pursue the son, Ian Bishop, because he hadn't shown any interest in the gospel. I wanted to visit the Bishop family, mainly to satisfy my own curiosity, but my trainer said it would be a waste of time.

When my trainer finished his mission, I got a new companion from the MTC. I thought to myself, "Well, there is no reason why we can't visit the Bishop family now." We set up the visit, and I remember coming away very impressed with Ian Bishop. I thought he was the brightest member of his family. He seemed very serious and thoughtful.

The Spirit told us to get to know Ian and not to talk about the gospel yet. Ian had an interest in cars. During our second visit to the family, we spent most of the time having Ian teach us how a car works. I was definitely lost but was amazed by his knowledge. I thought, "This young man is very diligent and studious about things that he cares about."

Because we took an interest in what Ian was interested in, he started to open up with us and asked us a lot of thoughtful questions about the gospel. He took a very strong interest in the Book of Mormon and the gospel in general. We started to teach Ian the lessons. I was soon transferred and my trainee and his new companion continued the lessons. Later, my trainee was transferred and Ian continued to study and pray about what he was learning. He was baptized several months after my transfer.

My current job takes me all over the world, so I was able to track down Ian after twenty-six years. We met at a restaurant in London, and his mother and his wife joined us. Ian not only joined the Church, but he also served on a mission in central England. He was married in the London England Temple and has four kids that he and his spouse are raising in the gospel. His oldest son is serving a mission in Pocatello, Idaho.

I often marvel what would have happened to Ian Bishop if we had not shown an interest in his car and in his life. What if we hadn't listened to the promptings of the Spirit to *not* talk about the gospel quite yet, sensing that the time would come when Ian would show an interest in the gospel and become a great contributor to the Church in England.

When I received my call to the England London South Mission, my family was excited. My father was especially excited because he had served in this same mission thirty years earlier. My mother was also enthused about the call but at the same time had a serious concern. She told me that the English people would be appalled with my table manners, or lack thereof. She had to reteach me how to eat and how to hold my knife and fork and made a long list of many things that I needed to stop or start doing.

As a good prospective missionary, I listened to my mother and painfully relearned and enhanced my table manners. Thanks to her, I can say that my manners probably didn't draw attention. But what my mom did not anticipate is that I would spend more than half of my mission working in South London. South London has a lot of immigrants from all over the world. Some of my favorite immigrants were those who came from Nigeria. They were always pleasant and humble people who were willing to hear the word of God.

I will never forget one moment in particular when I was eating fufu with twenty or so Nigerian people in a small flat in central London. Fufu is like sticky mashed potatoes that you eat with your hands. You pick up the fufu and dip it into several sauces (most of them are very spicy) and you are good to go. As my companion and I were dipping our hands into the fufu with our Nigerian brothers and sisters, the thought came to me: *If my mother could see me now!* My manners hadn't improved! In fact, they had gotten worse. But as I have explained, it is better to follow the spirit of the law, not the letter of the law when prompted. Getting to know and understand the Nigerian culture required me to eat like them even if it meant eating with my fingers. If I had refused to eat like them I would have alienated them, and I would not have had the opportunity to help them become members of Christ's church.

But I loved the Nigerians. Sometimes I felt that my mission was in Africa, since I spent so much time teaching these good people. I was fortunate to be able to baptize many of them. One of these people was Lou Akinrojumu, who was baptized along with her mother and siblings. Lou was a leader in her family and in the gospel. She became one of the first Nigerian sister missionaries serving in England. Later, she was married in the temple and is now raising a righteous family in the gospel. I'm glad that in this instance I didn't practice the good table manners my mother had so diligently taught me, otherwise I would have never eaten fufu, and if I never had eaten fufu I would have never met Lou.

My son Jacob is currently serving in the Australia Adelaide Mission. This location is a perfect fit for my son since he is so laid back and happy-go-lucky. I could not think of a more inspired call. Recently, in his letter, Jacob commented,

> You should see the humans I talk to everyday: a seven-foot-tall Sudanese man with a crucifix necklace, a whole gang of drunk Aboriginals on the bus, an Aussie businessman in an Armani suit. Elder Tsang (my Chinese companion) and I talk to every last one of them . . . The entire human family is here in the city. In the past three days, I've met someone from India, Congo, China, Japan, South Korea, Vietnam, Tonga, Fiji, Brazil, Belarus, Germany, Holland, Iran, Egypt, Afghanistan, France, Italy, and Hungary.

This was particularly interesting to me because Jacob had always shown a great interest in different people, cultures, and perspectives. He has had a very diverse upbringing. Born in Phoenix, Arizona, Jacob had lived in Boston, Massachusetts; Greenwich, Connecticut; Brisbane, Australia; Tokyo, Japan; and London, England all by the age of ten. Jacob has visited many states and more than twenty foreign countries. When he got to Australia, he wasn't thrown off by the diversity he encountered. On the contrary, he relished the opportunity to meet with so many different people. Jacob has a gift (given from God) to be natural, spontaneous, and fun with diverse people and in a variety of settings. It is easy for him to be himself and let his personality shine forth.

My sister Jenny served in the England Manchester Mission. She served in Preston, England. In 1998, our family attended the Preston England Temple dedication. We were also able to have a dinner with several of Jenny's converts. Each convert spent ten to fifteen minutes describing their conversion story and Jenny's involvement in that story. A similar theme began to emerge out of their stories. The theme was Jenny's persistence and unwillingness to let any of these converts off the hook. As close as I can remember, here is a list of the phrases her converts said at the dinner we had together:

- "I tried to tell Sister Covey that I wasn't interested in taking the lessons anymore, but she wouldn't hear it. She told me that I hadn't got to the best parts yet and that I needed to keep listening."

- "I kept trying to tell Sister Covey that my family wouldn't be interested in hearing the lessons, but she insisted and I couldn't refuse her."

- "I told Sister Covey that I couldn't be baptized because of my fear of the water. But she told me that was nonsense and just plain stupid."

- "I wanted to tell Sister Covey I wasn't going to invite my family to the baptism, but she continued to insist that I introduce her and her companion to my family. I didn't want to offend her, and knowing that she would not relent, I decided to comply."

Jenny's personality was one of persistence and persuasion. She simply would not accept no as an answer, and she would just continue to sweetly insist and persist until she got what she wanted. Well, this encouraged a lot of these English people out of their comfort zones, which prompted them to really study and pray about the doctrine they were receiving. And when they did, they gained powerful testimonies of the restored gospel. They were all happy that Jenny persisted, even though at the time they thought she was rather pushy.

I will never forget this dinner and how impressed I was with Jenny's converts. What if Jenny hadn't been Jenny? What if Jenny hadn't let her personality shine forth? I'm certain most of these fine people would not be members of the Church. I know this because many of them said so that night.

The whole point I'm making is that God is in charge. He knows the area in the world where each of his missionaries can have the most influence and impact. Our Heavenly Father knows our unique gifts and capacities. He is going to put us where He needs us to advance His purposes and to reach the people He has prepared for us. Are you letting your personality shine forth as a missionary? If not, you are missing a very important ingredient in your success as a missionary. Your personality may be the difference between whether someone investigates the gospel or chooses not to.

My son Jacob summarizes the balance he is trying to achieve on his mission:

> I've been having a lot of fun in my missionary work lately. I think every missionary has to deal with the great and eternal dilemma of finding where being your fun, silly self ends and where the quiet dignity of being a solemn representative of Jesus Christ begins. You must have both if you want anyone to 1) listen to you in the first place, and 2) feel the Spirit when you teach. Too much of one (being so serious that people yell "three cheers for sin" when you walk by) will result in the downfall of the other (if you're having too much fun, the Spirit won't bear witness of your words), so it is our monumental task to find where the two meet and both your personality and your solemn spirit work as one in bringing about conversion.

Now in fairness, I served my mission in an English-speaking country. I did not need to learn a language. It can be much harder to let your personality shine forth when you can hardly speak the language or carry on a gospel conversation. To this I would say, be patient and know that, in time, your language skills will improve so that you will be able to not only converse and bear testimony but also let your personality shine forth in a foreign tongue.

■ ■ ■

The Growing Impact of Sister Missionaries

Today, with the recent announcement by President Monson lowering the age for sister missionaries to nineteen, we have seen a huge influx of sisters joining the missionary force. Some estimate that sister missionaries will make up one-third to one-half of the missionary force in the world, whereas before the announcement, sister missionaries made up 5 to 10 percent.

I am personally surrounded by sister missionaries. My two older sisters served in Ireland, and two of my younger sisters served in England. My wife served in Barcelona, Spain, and her mother served in Germany twice, the first time as a sister missionary and later with her husband. I have witnessed firsthand the incredible impact sisters missionaries make and continue to make.

President Spencer W. Kimball said prophetically in 1979, "Thus it will be that the female exemplars of the Church will be a significant force in both the numerical and the spiritual growth of the Church in the last days" (Women's Conference September 15, 1979, *Ensign*, October, 1979). What an exciting and truly historic time we live in today. Perhaps President Kimball was given a glimpse into the future of the contribution sisters missionaries will make in convert baptisms. My wife's story illustrates this point.

> I recall meeting Alicia upon being transferred to Badalona on the outskirts of Barcelona. She was in her late thirties with two young daughters and a husband named Ramon, who made his living as a taxi driver. Alicia ran her own business as a seamstress so I felt an instant connection, as I too love to sew. Alicia seemed more a member than many of the members in the Badalona ward. She

attended church meetings, participated in Relief Society, and was as active as anyone. The surprising fact was that in thirteen years of investigating, she had never agreed to baptism.

As we became acquainted, I was determined to discover what was holding her back. Our lessons went smoothly, [and] she believed in the teachings we shared and kept her commitments—aside from being baptized. After building rapport thru several lessons, I asked how it was she had been investigating for so long and not joined yet. She replied that often she had to work on Sunday, that she hadn't felt she could open up to the many companionships of elders thru the years, that her husband had opposed it, and a variety of other excuses that didn't seem to totally fit. I wondered if we shouldn't stop teaching her, surely in thirteen years she had had ample opportunity to embrace the truth.

I felt impressed to continue teaching her, this time involving her young daughters who had not really participated in the lessons and commitments previously. The girls became very engaged and soon wanted to be baptized. Alicia consented, but refused to join them. I prayed to understand why. I was training a greenie at the time. We went to visit her one evening, and Alicia was in tears. Rather than blaze thru the lesson we had planned, I just listened as Alicia unloaded the pain she was experiencing in her marriage. My companion looked anxious, because with her limited Spanish, she didn't understand what was happening. Where was the flip chart and why wasn't the lesson we had planned being taught?

Alicia, after calming down, finally confided that she would not be baptized without her husband, because she felt that if she did, there would be a rift in their relationship. If they didn't get baptized together, he would never follow. I came away elated with the progress. We finally knew what was holding her back! But my well-intended, letter-of-the-law greenie reported me to the mission president for wasting time and for "just being a friend." The president called me to repentance, but when I explained the context and what had transpired that night with Alicia, he became totally supportive.

We finally had an answer that made sense as to how to progress this family! In all those years of the missionaries coming to their home, Ramon had never participated. He allowed his wife, and now his girls, but he did not want any part of it. We now had a clear-cut goal and began to seek out opportunities to involve Ramon in the lessons and FHEs. We began to build a relationship with him. We found he liked to cook; I expressed an interest in learning to cook from him. He taught us how to make Spanish dishes like paella, aioli, and crema Catalan. He became surprisingly open and began to participate in the lessons, much to the delight of his wife and daughters. He attended the girls' baptism and began to be fellowshipped by ward members. His major roadblock in the conversion process was smoking, but with the help of the Lord and our enthusiastic support, he was able to overcome that addiction at that time.

The day Alicia and Ramon entered the waters of baptism was a joy. Over several months, the entire family, including Alicia's mother, were able to join the Church. Once they felt understood and supported, with their concerns resolved, they were each able to embrace the gospel and enter in the straight and narrow path that leads to eternal life.

Each of us that enters in to the service of the Lord to serve a full-time mission has certain people that can be reached specifically by us. Somehow we will have just what they need to open up and overcome their concerns and fears. We will have the testimony that will touch their hearts. We will be able to help them feel and recognize the Spirit witnessing to the truth of our message. Never underestimate your ability to bless lives as you boldly serve and share the unique gifts you have been given for the Lord's divine purposes."

In my own mission, I also noticed that faithful and hard-working sisters missionaries had phenomenal success wherever they went. What is it about the sister missionaries that allows them to reach people that the elders often can't? I attribute it to three unique attributes:

First, sisters are less intimidating. One of the main reasons a missionary does not make it past the front door and into the home is that the homeowner feels nervous about letting strangers in. However, women are less threatening than men and thereby have an easier time getting invited into homes. My wife, Pamelyn, relates, "I met a woman named Gloria while tracting in Badalona, Spain. After letting my companion and me into her home, Gloria explained that many times elders had come knocking at her door, but she never felt comfortable letting them in. We were the first sisters to ring her bell. She allowed us in and was very curious about our message. Soon thereafter she and her five children were baptized."

Second, sister missionaries often form emotional connections faster with investigators and members than elders do. Not to say that elders can't also accomplish this, but my experience has been that people let their emotional guard down easier with women and tend to trust them faster. This emotional connection is especially crucial in the beginning of a relationship when trying to get people to make and keep their commitments. This connection can also be enhanced when the investigators have little children.

Finally, women tend to be more nurturing and compassionate listeners than most men. This quality greatly helps when teaching investigators who want to share deeply personal experiences and need someone to empathetically listen in order to understand where they are coming from.

I am thrilled that the age of the sister missionary has been changed to nineteen! I personally believe it will lead to more success, more baptisms, and more converted missionaries in the future. Today's missionary army using both the power of the priesthood in its elders combined with the goodness of the sister missionaries will be an unstoppable force for good!

■ ■ ■

Chapter 7 Questions

1. Do I follow the Spirit when it directs me to follow an unorthodox path while teaching investigators and potential investigators?

2. Do my investigators know I love and care for them regardless of their interest in the gospel?

3. Has my personality been subdued on my mission? Am I letting my personality shine forth?

4. Have I achieved a balance on my mission of being a solemn representative of the Lord Jesus Christ but also having fun and not taking myself too seriously?

5. Do I see examples in my everyday missionary life where my unique skills, attributes, and personality align well with the history, culture, and peoples of my mission?

6. Can I see ways where I can let my personality shine forth more? Do I think this approach will help me become a more effective missionary?

■ ■ ■

CHAPTER 8:

Closing

"I know that which the Lord hath commanded me, and I glory in it. I do not glory of myself, but I glory in that which the Lord hath commanded me; yea, and this is my glory, that perhaps I may be an instrument in the hands of God to bring some soul to repentance; and this is my joy. And behold, when I see many of my brethren truly penitent, and coming to the Lord their God, then is my soul filled with joy." (Alma 29:9–10)

■ ■ ■

My intent in writing this book is to inspire more missionaries to be productive and effective and to make significant contributions. This will result in more people becoming members of Christ's church. Much of what I've shared in this book I learned from my father. He taught me the importance of becoming a highly effective missionary and instrument in the hands of the Lord. He taught me that often missionaries become robotic, go through the motions, and get stuck in mediocre habits. He helped me recognize that I needed to constantly step outside my comfort zone and push and challenge myself in order to achieve breakthroughs.

In many ways, this book reflects his teachings to me. My father spoke from experience. He opened up the Belfast Ireland Mission and saw two thousand baptisms during his three years as mission president. It took another thirty years and ten mission presidents to add the next two thousand baptisms in Ireland. Spencer W. Kimball once said of my father while visiting him in the field: "He is the most effective missionary in the Church today." Quite a compliment coming from a missionary giant like President Kimball!

Yes, it is true that people have the agency to accept or reject the gospel message, but it is also true that our level of instrumentality depends on us. When we are more prepared and apply the principles of baptism, the Lord can do great things through us. In reference to His miracles, the Savior said to His disciples, "Greater works than these shall you do" (John 14:12).

I ask you to apply the approaches that lead to being a highly effective missionary and abandon those that don't work. Are some approaches contained in this book not suited to your mission? Possibly. But keep in mind it is your role as a missionary to come up with new and different approaches that enable breakthroughs. I have no doubt if I were a full-time missionary now, I would come back with several new insights and approaches beyond what is currently contained in this book.

The real question to ask yourself is, How effective do I want to be as a missionary? If you are already highly effective, then by all means please keep doing what you're doing. It's working. But if you are not as effective as you know you can be, then perhaps some of these approaches are worth trying. Whether it is through the application of the ideas contained in this book or through your own experience of trial and error, I'm advocating being as highly effective as possible in moving this great work forward.

Missionaries should never lose sight of their purpose. That purpose is clearly stated on page 1 in *Preach My Gospel*: "Invite others to come unto Christ by helping them receive the restored gospel through faith in Jesus Christ and His Atonement, repentance, baptism, receiving the gift of the Holy Ghost, and enduring to the end."

Preach My Gospel also answers the question: How will I know whether I am a successful missionary? It states: "Your success as a missionary is measured primarily by your commitment to find, teach, baptize, and confirm people and to help them become faithful members of the Church who enjoy the presence of the Holy Ghost" (10).

I'm amazed at God's hand in the conversion process. In the summer of 2012, my seventeen-year-old daughter, Jacquelyn, spent three weeks in Thailand doing humanitarian service. While there, she had the opportunity to share the gospel to some of her coparticipants. One of Jacquelyn's best friends on that trip was a young woman named Stephanie Parsons from Montreal, Canada. Jacquelyn introduced the gospel to Stephanie and referred the missionaries to Stephanie upon her return to Canada. Stephanie took the missionary lessons, read the Book of Mormon, attended church, gained a testimony, and was baptized. I was honored to baptize and confirm her a member of the church. At the end of her baptism service, Stephanie gave a powerful testimony (her story follows below). What struck me most about Stephanie's story was how her life experiences had prepared her to embrace the gospel. Jacquelyn was merely an instrument in God's hands to help Stephanie recognize the truths that He had been teaching her along the way. Here is her remarkable conversion story, which she delivered at her baptismal service in Montreal, Canada:

My journey to this moment began with a twelve-year-old Buddhist monk in the opposite corner of the world. It was truly what could be described as none other than a miraculous and divine quilt of meaningful coincidences. Or, as I have come to realize, what became, when sewn together, far more than simply just coincidences.

I want to quickly rewind to 2011. It's my high school graduation and I'm voted most likely to raise six kids on a farm. Fact: this was indeed nothing less than a dream I have always carried with me in the back of my mind. Or, if we're being honest, the front! I often dreamed of my six beautiful children who would fill the house with pattering feet as I got everybody ready to walk down the road to church every Sunday. But, I had to come to terms with the fact that this idealized life would live forever trapped in my imagination. Supposedly, that type of life just didn't exist in this century. But I prayed about it, to a God that I had never introduced myself to. But I knew He was there. I needed Him to be.

Fast-forward one year. I'm in Thailand surrounded by the lush greenery and infinite rice fields. Sitting in the airport on our very first day, I could have sworn I overheard this brave blonde girl courageously tell our entire group of strangers that she was a Mormon. But no, I must have misheard, I thought. No more than twenty-four hours into the trip, it seemed as if this Mormon creature and I were connecting over her missionary letters, and her worn scripture set stared at me from her headboard. The Church often came up in conversation amongst our group, while squatting in rivers picking up rocks, and the way that Jacquelyn spoke so passionately about her beliefs attracted new people to learn everyday. It was on the fifth night in our paradise, when Jacquelyn invited me to read the history of Joseph Smith, that I knew this was far more than an attractive lifestyle to me. With a mosquito net pitched over my head and farm animals conversing with the moon, a dim flashlight illuminated her pages long after the rest of the group had fallen asleep. I read of how Joseph Smith was a confused teenage boy who didn't know which Church to join in a time period when new Christian churches were being born every day. It astonished me that I could feel so intimately connected to this history and the struggle that Joseph Smith had. I felt like, on an obviously more subtle level, Joseph Smith's religious journey was exactly the one that I had always been overwhelmed by. I figured that, if praying about it worked for him, then I had nothing to lose. Eight days later, I journaled that "some gut feeling tells me I am supposed to be Mormon."

If I have gained a testimony of one thing throughout this journey, it is that our Heavenly Father honestly and truly looks after us and guides us through our trials and doubts. Thailand became my safe place; an entire country where I could sit and openly read the Book of Mormon, avoid criticisms about being the forever "designated driver," and know that I could always look to my side, see Jacquelyn, and know that if I ever lacked the faith, she had more than enough to go around.

As our trip days dwindled down, and my faith and testimony of the Church was constantly challenged as I stressed about returning home, we headed to our last service project in an isolated Thai elementary school. Let me stress the word *isolated*. We were the only moving vehicles within miles, and we hadn't seen another Western person in hours. Yet somehow, we ran into a group of missionaries. Although they were not from our Church, and they didn't share which Christian denomination they were from, this young boy by the name of Nate approached Jacquelyn and I on a picnic bench. He told of how he was once into drugs and alcohol and then one day he felt inclined to go to church and was completely saved. This boy was exactly my age at the time. He asked Jacquelyn and I if we knew Christ and, although Jacquelyn responded with confidence, I simply said, "I'm working on it." As Nate walked away, I felt an impulse to ask him where he was from. Believe it or not, he was from none other than tiny Kingston, Ontario, merely a few blocks from my new home at Queens University.

Honestly, I'm no superwoman, and going home felt like a spiritual tornado. I spent hours upon hours with Elder Holbrook and Elder Baker, delving into the scriptures. Of course, they invited me to read Moroni's promise, and they assured me that I would get the same answer they had. I agreed, but was skeptical that I would have to make up some magical religious experience as my answer. The night of my eighteenth birthday party, I was dragged out to a club to "celebrate," and was overwhelmed by the suddenly unattractive scene before me. That night, more confused than ever, I pondered my scriptures and spoke to my friends about the Church. We spoke of happiness and I felt this feeling so purely and deeply that it was overwhelming. I woke up with a feeling I had never before felt in my life. My soul felt tangibly higher and freer while I felt grounded in my life plans and my present goals and experiences. I did not feel constricted or weighed down anymore. My heart and soul seemed to be weightless, floating above the world's problems and simply looking on in harmony and legitimate happiness. It was in this peaceful feeling that I knew I had my real, authentic answer to Moroni's promise. I knew it then, and I know it now with every bone in my body, that this Church is true. And I know that our Heavenly Father planned this entire journey out meticulously for me.

However, this journey was never an easy path. The night after I felt the power and truth of the Church, I journaled of how my friends and family would never support this and how I should forget everything I had felt. But, once again, our Heavenly Father knew of my troubles and he sent me the most beautiful stranger to hold my hand. The very next day, after expressing my new doubts, I was sitting on the metro when an African woman, dressed all in orange, with green mascara and giant hoop earrings, approached my friends and me and encouraged us to pursue happiness. But then, she directed her attention directly on me, as if nobody else existed in that moment, and she asked if I was Christian. When I nodded, she asked me if I would follow her in prayer. I repeated after her, "Jesus, come into my heart, forgive me all my sins and accept me into your kingdom. Thank you, Jesus." She smiled at me and left the metro car. I sat on the grass in the Old Port and journaled that it would be impossible to have experienced such things, and be surrounded by such beauty everyday, if our Heavenly Father didn't exist.

But I was about to uproot every connection to the Church that

I had established by moving to Kingston and being thrown into the infamous week of 24/7 drunkenness known as Frosh Week. I remember calling Jacquelyn less than forty-eight hours after move-in and telling her that something felt very internally wrong about my new home. I was spiritually and emotionally confused. Jacquelyn gave the best advice she knew how and told me to have patience, to give it a chance, and she left me promising that she had been and would continue to pray for me. In all honesty, I thought that praying from another country would definitely not help my situation here in dreadful drunk Kingston. But again, our Heavenly Father knew the righteous desires of my heart. He felt the struggle that I was having and, even though he had helped me gain a testimony many times over. He lent me his hand once again. Just hours after I hung up the phone with Jacquelyn, I left for my faculty formal. My faculty at Queen's is notorious for being extremely small, with less than two hundred people, and we were split up into small frosh groups of ten people. I sat down at a table with some friends I had made in my group but was advised by my leader to move to a new table and meet new people because, this time last year, she had met people on this night that had changed her life. Skeptical, as always, I agreed and sat amongst total strangers and casually engaged in small talk. Out of the corner of my ear, I overheard one of my new friends talking about a boy in her frosh group who was twenty-two and "so old." A feeling inside of me prompted me to include myself in this conversation and I abruptly asked her why he was so old. She casually responded that he had just returned from a church mission. I do believe my heart stopped in that moment. I knew that this was none other than The Church of Jesus Christ of Latter-day Saints, and I asked that she introduce us. I met Scott, who proudly introduced me to yet another church member who was in our faculty. Together, we scouted the dance floor, and he eventually found none other than Rachel. Rachel had been with me for the past two days, all day, because she was assigned, out of the thousands of Queen's freshman students, to be in my exact same frosh group of ten people! I suppose you can say that this is how I came to have a strong testimony of the power of prayer.

Throughout the first months of school, I found so many blessing by following the Word of Wisdom and practicing our faith. The friends that I made were genuine and not just drunk stories to tell through the morning-after hangover. But there was nothing that pushed me through the first semester more than my countdown to visit Jacquelyn and her family in Utah over American Thanksgiving.

Come November, no matter how hard I tried to avoid it, I fell in love with the feeling that Utah gave me. We skipped from the Temple to the Joseph Smith Memorial Building and we ended, on our last day together, in her family ward for sacrament meeting. It was surreal to be able to pass the sacrament over to Jacquelyn's hand, the one who had sparked this whole journey. And then, by some strange "coincidence," the speakers that day stood up and announced that they had just returned from serving a mission . . . in Montreal! They spoke of the Montreal Temple that I drove by so frequently when clearing my head, and of the amazing members, which I could picture in my mind as friends. Jacquelyn's dad was teaching the Sunday School class on Mormon 1–6, so we stayed to listen. At the beginning of the lesson he asked if there were any visitors, and he had Jacquelyn introduce me to everyone. David then said that it was odd that I came all the way from Montreal to hear a sacrament meeting full of talks about Montreal, something he said was 'truly no coincidence' at all. I am inclined to agree.

And so here I am. I know that the people in the Book of Mormon actually lived and knew Christ even as I live and know Christ. I know that Joseph Smith was a true prophet of God. I know that God is the Father and that he loves us to no end. I know that His Son Jesus Christ lived and died so that you and I can one day return to our heavenly home. And it is with every ounce of my being that I can say that this book has changed my life. I say these things in the name of Jesus Christ. Amen."

In conclusion, I hope this book will serve as a catalyst to help you:

- ■ See key indicators (numbers) as "Christlike service to your fellowmen."

- ■ Apply the principles of baptisms every day.

- ■ Implement effective personal contacting approaches. Much of your success as a missionary will come through your own efforts in partnership with God.

- ■ Become a pillar of strength in helping your investigators make and keep commitments. Only through commitments can the work of conversion move forward.

- Significantly involve the members in the work so that they can fulfill their important role and you can see the work dramatically advanced.

- Continuously look to achieve breakthroughs and become a more productive missionary.

- Become an effective instrument in the hands of God by sharing the gospel with all those you come in contact with. I have no doubt there are many more Stephanie Parsonses out there.

You have been reserved to teach the gospel in this day and age. I pray for your success every day. I know you can do it. Here's to you becoming a highly effective missionary!

David M. R. Covey
June 2013

■■■ Appendix ■■■

Survey Questionnaire

1. Is a close, strong family important to you?

2. Should churches provide better programs for families and youth?

3. Do you have a belief in God?

4. Do you believe in Jesus Christ as the Son of God?

5. Have you ever asked yourself questions like, "Where did I come from?" "Why am I here on earth?" and "Where will I go after I die?" Do you think that there are answers to these questions?

6. Do you believe the Bible to be the word of God or just a history book? If you knew there was another book of scripture written by prophets that testifies of Christ, would you read it?

7. Do you pray?

8. If so, do you feel that God hears and answers prayers?

9. How do you cope with a crisis in your life?

10. Would you like to be happier than you are now? What would make you happier?

1								
2								
3								
4								
5								
6								
7								
8								
9								
10								

■ ■ ■

Placing the Book of Mormon

The idea behind this approach is to present the book in such a way that it appears to be of great worth (which it is). Let's say you have an antique vase you want to show to a friend. It's priceless—it's been in the family for many, many years. You would naturally be hesitant to let go of it, even for just the few minutes that your friend will be handling it. So, you'll hand it over with great care, making sure they know how much it means to you.

Well, placing the Book of Mormon should be much the same. After you've explained the book and expressed your own feelings about what it means to you, you'll carefully give them the book as a meaningful gift to be treasured (and read!). Below is a simple example of one way to present the Book of Mormon:

(Holding the book with both hands) "Mr. Hutchings, I'd like to share with you something that means so much to me! As I mentioned, this book will bring you closer to your Heavenly Father. I know, because I've grown closer myself through reading and applying its principles." (Start to hand the book to him, and then slowly withdraw it back to yourself). "You know, it's very important that you read and ponder the message for yourself—come to know for yourself, like I have, that these things are true . . ." (Again, slowly hand over the book, and hesitantly bring it back). "Will you be sure to pray about the things you discover? I know you will. Please let me know how you feel about the things you read." (Now, surrender the book. By this time, if it's done right, they will snatch it out of your hands and be quite excited to find out what it's all about).

The difference between just handing a copy to someone after an explanation and meaningfully sharing it with someone will really help them to see the importance of it and want to read and study it.

You may also use the "Curiosity" approach. After you've explained the book and a few of its teachings, leave the book with them with the challenge to read just the introduction and nothing else! Say, "Whatever you do, don't read past the introduction until we return, okay?" Now, what do you suppose they're going to do? Of course—they'll be curious to find out what's beyond the introduction page and will begin to read on ahead.

■ ■ ■

Callback Dialogue— What to Say

This section gives some examples of what to say when you go to visit a callback off the questionnaire. You'll want to approach with the knowledge that the person you're coming to see has already said they want to know more. There's no need to ask questions such as, "Are you still interested?" because they already said they are. Rather, be fully positive and enthusiastic and say something like: "Hello, Mr. Leavitt! It's good to see you again. May we come in?"

Now you may think at first that this approach is quite bold, but it really works! Just have the confidence that the callback is an "old friend" who would love to have you over to share a lesson, and you'll be successful. It's also so quick that it seems natural to invite you in, so they will. If the person can't remember taking the questionnaire, or asks why you want to come in, say:

"I'm Sister _____, and this is Sister _____. You helped us out last Saturday in town by answering a few questions about your family and some of your basic beliefs. We would like to share with you a little more about the questionnaire, and we have a great message that goes along with it. Would you be so kind as to let us in so we could share that with you?"

At times the person you questioned may give you an incorrect address. If that occurs, always take a questionnaire with the person who lives at the incorrect address. Try something like: "Hello, sir! The other day we took a brief questionnaire with Mrs. _____, and she gave us permission to call on her again. Is she in?" (No, she doesn't live here.) "We must have gotten an incorrect address, but say! We're sure glad you're home. So we didn't make an unnecessary journey, could you help us out with this questionnaire?" (Then use the rest of the 8-Step Door Approach.)

Possibly the person you call back on isn't quite as interested as they were when you questioned them. If that happens, show extra enthusiasm and get them to feel the same excitement you had when you talked with them on the street. Try saying something like, "Remember how interesting this questionnaire was and the question you had about why we're here on earth? Well, this message we have today only takes about fifteen minutes and will answer that question you have, as well as many others! May we please come in and share it with you?"

Also, the person with whom you took the questionnaire may not be home, but try something like this to the person that is home: "Hello, ma'am! We took this short questionnaire with John the day before yesterday, and he was very interested in what we asked him. We surely would like your help as well. Could we come in to take the questionnaire with you?"

■ ■ ■

Question and Answer with President John F. Grove

A year after returning from my mission, I had the opportunity to talk with John F. Grove about my mission experiences as well as the missionary contacting and committing approaches we applied in the ELSM. John was a convert to the Church and had joined the Church in his mid-twenties in York, Pennsylvania. He asked my mission president, Ed Pinegar, who was currently serving as the Provo MTC President, advice on what he should do as a new mission president. President Pinegar referred him to me. This was the first time I had the privilege of meeting with President Grove as he prepared for his assignment in the Montana Billings Mission.

I was able on three different occasions to train John and all of his missionaries in the philosophy and approaches we used in the ELSM. I spent two full weeks in his mission. John was a fast learner and implementer. During his term as mission president, from July 1988 to June 1991, the Montana Billings Mission (MBM) achieved the following results:

- 806 Baptisms in calendar year 1989 (surpassing the previous high of 802 in 1982)

- 1,155 Baptisms in 1990 (smashing the 1989 record)

- Average discussions in the mission went from 120 per week in August 1988 to an average of 1,200 per week during the last 18 months of his mission, with a high of 1,352 discussions in one week.

- In January 1991, the mission broke the monthly baptism record with 139 baptisms (previous records were 127 in January 1990 and before that, 112 in March 1981)

■ The Montana Billings Mission became one of the top baptizing missions in the Church compared to all English-speaking missions in 1990 and the first half of 1991.

Because this is my best example, other than my own mission, of a mission that fully implemented all the approaches and ideas contained in my book, I have included a question-and-answer section with President Grove that contains the questions I am most frequently asked when I teach my book's approach to missionaries and mission presidents.

1. Why did you choose to implement the ideas and approaches contained in David's book?

President Grove: I am and always have been excited by the way the Lord gives you the basic program and then allows you the opportunity to use your own approach as to how you carry out your calling. About two months prior to our mission, my wife and I visited with several former mission presidents in order to learn from them why they were so successful. One on these presidents knew of the great success David had had on his mission and suggested that I may want to talk to him. I did not know David but accepted this suggestion. Wow, was I impressed with his approach. On top of that, the statistics were there to confirm how well they worked. Since none of this was in writing, I took lots of notes and was in very close contact with David in the early days of our mission.

Also, I am a great believer in getting to know where the person's "mind-set" is before giving them my message. David's approach gave us the opportunity to do just that. Thus, I really wanted to learn all I could about the approach and also have my key leaders do the same.

2. How did you implement the ideas contained in David's book?

President Grove:

A. We worked very hard in personally training the missionaries. We got leadership "buy-in" from the top down. My assistants and zone leaders were convinced that if they learned and practiced this whole system, success would follow.

B. We set mission goals that focused on the most important behaviors, such as lessons taught in a day and week and so on.

C. I used my interviews to reinforce those behaviors.

D. We focused on those behaviors in our prayers.

E. We taught the program the moment the new missionaries landed at the airport. It became part of all of us. We focused on questions that investigators would most likely say yes to.

3. What resistance did you find after David presented his system to the missionaries in your mission?

President Grove: Very little. Missionaries who were not interested in performance and measurements didn't fight it out right and frankly were in the minority. My predecessor focused on obedience and living by the Spirit, which made it more probable that these missionaries were ready to take off and perform.

The program clearly represented cultural change, and all for the better, I might add. Very quickly results began to roll in that helped those who may have resisted otherwise. Quickly they began to realize that this was not going away. Repetition helped us to get all on board. All zone conferences, interviews, leadership meetings focused on the program. Missionaries who were not naturally bold had to learn some new skills, which, frankly, most did.

4. What did you do to resolve the concerns of those missionaries that resisted adopting David's approach? How long did it take to resolve their concerns?

President Grove: As I said previously, those that fought this approach were few. I focused on training the mission zone and district leaders and since the program was the way we all lived and talked this was not a big point with us. However, we were good listeners and assisted those who had problems by being attentive to their concerns and along with them found things they could do that fit with their personality and way of doing things. This helped quite a bit.

For the first few months, we had a team of traveling zone leaders who covered the mission, teaching and paying attention to concerns and helping resolve them.

Our first General Authority mission tour was by our Area President, Loren C. Dunn. What he taught us seemed to go hand and hand with David's approach. Things like getting them to their knees in prayer, being bold yet kind. He also stressed the Soft Challenge in the first discussion and always challenging for baptism by the end of the second discussion. He also stressed the importance of spending your time with good prospects versus carrying investigators because you enjoyed visiting them. David's program went hand in hand with what Elder Dunn taught.

5. How long did it take for the contacting approaches (survey questionnaire) to begin working mission-wide?

President Grove: First of all we called it our contacting approach, rather than that we were taking a survey. It took about three to four months to get this going mission-wide, and then it simply grew and got better and better as the weeks went by.

6. How long did it take for the committing approaches (Soft Challenge, Straight-Gate Dialogue, and the Commitment Dialogue) to begin working mission-wide?

President Grove: With many of the missionaries, they started using the whole program early on. I would say that the majority of the mission was using the approaches after three to four months. It is important to note that this was a growing process during those early months with many of the missionaries using everything during the first month or two. The whole mission was on track in less than six months.

7. What adjustments or modifications did you make to the materials/approaches you learned from David? Did the changes you made improve things?

President Grove: We didn't use the word *survey* nor did we imply that the questions we were asking were being tallied. We simply were asking the questions to learn their thoughts on the things we were asking about. Usually the changes we made were subtle and were made to assist missionaries to feel they had input in the process, which indeed they did.

8. **Your time as a mission president ended twenty-two years ago. Are the ideas and approaches in this book still relevant? If so, why?**

President Grove: Absolutely! I counseled with several of my assistants in a conference call to insure that my thoughts were in line. They jumped right on this. One said that serving as a ward mission leader he used the challenge process, and it increased the baptismal success in his ward. All of them, including me, answered very positively to this question. We really need a program like this in our missionary work today.

9. **If you were a new mission president, what would be the best way to implement these ideas/approaches in concert with the mission-wide church guidebook *Preach My Gospel*?**

President Grove: I see them going hand in hand. Here are a few thoughts on that.

- Both approaches focus on building relationships of trust.

- Asking questions and then listening go hand in hand with both approaches. People respond much better if they feel they are being listened to. I know when I was investigating the gospel I was overwhelmed by what the Bible said about what my missionary was teaching me. I was in awe with what was in the Bible.

- I would carefully work with my assistants and zone leaders to ensure they are on board. If not, I would consult the Lord to assist me in making some changes.

10. Anything else you would like to share or point out?

President Grove: David's program would most likely change the way a mission approaches missionary work. It would be helpful to drive that point home as an alert to the missionaries to expect it to be different.

- Be prepared to follow up, follow up, follow up. This needs to be taught, retaught and retaught. As we all know, new programs often go by the board and some of the missionaries may think they can wait to change because they think, "this too will pass."

- Be sure to use the soft challenge at the conclusion of the first lesson.

- Be sure to use the Strait-Gate Dialogue at the end of the second lesson.

- Focus on teaching skills to start a conversation. The old common ones don't work well. Again, well-thought questions are the key.

- Many of the Brethren teach us to rely on our knowledge if the Spirit doesn't give you specific answers to your concerns on the next step. Remember you are taught to follow the leadership of your mission president, and if he teaches you to do something, then do it unless the Spirit specifically demands it, and that likely will not happen. A missionary will likely be amazed at what following the program brings to him or her by doing so and the results will likely be very positive!

- This last one is a big one. President Monson has taught us that "When performance is measured, performance improves." I add that when it is fed back in a timely fashion, it has the overall greatest effect. One of the keys to our success was my weekly letter to the missionaries. One highly effective mission president told me that because he expected a weekly letter from the missionaries, he owes them a weekly letter. I sent the missionaries a weekly letter, which included feedback on their performance, and a short letter from me to them. This weekly feedback had a real positive effect on our success. With respect for the best missionary approach I have ever seen I submit this, my feedback.

John F. Grove, Jr.

Mission President, Montana Billings Mission, 1988–1991

About the Author

■ ■ ■

■ ■ ■

Born and raised into an incredible teaching and learning environment, David M. R. Covey naturally leaned toward teaching like his father, the late Stephen R. Covey. While serving as a missionary in the England London South Mission (ELSM), he quickly recognized the huge gap between the unsuccessful missionaries and the successful ones. It was not their lack of faith or desire, neither was it a lack of obedience to mission rules. All good missionaries had this. Instead, it was the lack of staying true to the proven principles that bring about baptism. Learning from a dynamic mission president and creative companions, David began to develop these skills and techniques, which dramatically increased his effectiveness as a missionary and as a result compounded his convert baptisms. Today, working as a business owner and entrepreneur, David loves to share his insights and approach to prospective missionaries and mission presidents whenever and wherever he can. David is married to his high school sweetheart, Pamelyn West Covey. David is the father of seven children: four boys and three girls.